CONGRESS AND THE LEGISLATIVE PROCESS

**FOUNDATIONS OF AMERICAN GOVERNMENT
AND POLITICAL SCIENCE**

Joseph P. Harris, Consulting Editor

Revisions and additions have been made to keep this series up to date and to enlarge its scope, but its purpose remains the same as it was on first publication: To provide a group of relatively short treatises dealing with major aspects of government in modern society. Each volume introduces the reader to a major field of political science through a discussion of important issues, problems, processes, and forces and includes at the same time an account of American political institutions. The author of each work is a distinguished scholar who specializes in and teaches the subjects covered. Together the volumes are well adapted to serving the needs of introductory courses in American government and political science.

ANDREW HACKER   The Study of Politics: The Western Tradition and American Origins

C. HERMAN PRITCHETT   The American Constitutional System, 3d ed.

HUGH A. BONE and AUSTIN RANNEY   Politics and Voters, 3d ed.

ROWLAND EGGER   The President of the United States, 2d ed.

JOSEPH P. HARRIS   Congress and the Legislative Process, 2d ed.

JOHN J. CORSON and JOSEPH P. HARRIS   Public Administration in Modern Society

CHARLES O. LERCHE, JR.   America in World Affairs, 2d ed.

CHARLES R. ADRIAN   Governing Our Fifty States and Their Communities, 3d ed.

H. FRANK WAY, JR.   Liberty in the Balance: Current Issues in Civil Liberties, 3d ed.

CONGRESS AND THE LEGISLATIVE PROCESS

SECOND EDITION

JOSEPH P. HARRIS
PROFESSOR OF POLITICAL SCIENCE, EMERITUS
UNIVERSITY OF CALIFORNIA, BERKELEY

McGRAW-HILL BOOK COMPANY

New York   San Francisco   St. Louis   Düsseldorf   Johannesburg
Kuala Lumpur   London   Mexico   Montreal   New Delhi   Panama
Rio de Janeiro   Singapore   Sydney   Toronto

This book was set in Helvetica by Rocappi, Inc., and printed on permanent paper and bound by George Banta Company. The designer was Janet Bollow. The editors were Robert P. Rainier and Michael A. Ungersma. Charles A. Goehring supervised production.

CONGRESS AND THE LEGISLATIVE PROCESS

Printed in the United States of America.

Library of Congress catalog card number: 78-172654

1234567890 BABA 798765432

PREFACE

This study describes the important features and operation of the Congress: the organization, political leadership, and procedures of each house; the role of the individual member and how he serves his constituents; the committee system and the rule of seniority; the customs and traditions of Congress; the role of the President as chief legislator; the conduct of investigations; the control of the purse; and proposed congressional reforms. In this edition, I have drawn heavily on the numerous excellent studies of Congress published by political scientists since 1967, when the first edition appeared. More than half of the volume has been entirely rewritten; many brief case studies and illustrative materials have been added. New sections have been added on the President as chief legislator, the 1970 Legislative Reorganization Act and the role of the congressman. The treatment of the House Rules Committee, the rule of seniority, and the congressional party system has been expanded and rewritten. Increased attention and emphasis have been given to legislative behavior throughout the study.

Since 1965, the movement for the improvement of congressional procedures and operations has continued, finally resulting in the passage of the Legislative Reorganization Act of 1970. This act provides for increased research services for Congress, substantially increases the staff allowances to members of the House of Representatives, adopts a number of procedural improvements in the work of committees, and creates a continuing joint committee on the organization of Congress. Probably the most important changes were the provision requiring committees to report roll-call votes and the change requiring teller votes in the House to be recorded by name when demanded by one-fifth of a quorum. These changes are intended to remove the veil of secrecy that has heretofore applied to committee votes and to votes in the House when in session as a committee of the whole to consider amendments. The result of these changes will be to make members more responsible to their constituents.

There is a continuing movement for improvements in Congress that will enable it to deal more promptly and effectively with the major problems of the country. Illustrative of this movement is the report of the Committee for Economic Development in 1970. The committee recommended changes in the committee system, including discontinuance of the rigid unwritten rule of seniority in selecting committee chairmen. It also recommended fundamental changes in congressional control of finance, and other reforms. There is a question, however, whether Congress can or will adopt the far-reaching changes in its organization and procedures urged upon it by the reformers.

The functions of the Congress, its role and importance to the nation, as well as the job, power, and prestige of the individual member and his opportunity for distinguished public service, have greatly increased and changed in the past 40 years. Congress has undergone significant changes and developments since the end of World War II. With a greatly increased and more professional staff, it is far better equipped today to perform its legislative functions than it was before

1945. Despite these developments, however, there are persistent criticisms of Congress for its inability or failure to deal effectively with the pressing problems confronting the nation, accompanied by demands for congressional reform. The purpose of this volume is to describe and explain Congress, its operations, and the legislative process. Knowledge of Congress and how it works is essential to an understanding of the American governmental and political institutions.

JOSEPH P. HARRIS

CONTENTS

CONGRESS AND THE LEGISLATIVE PROCESS

1 CONGRESS AND AMERICA'S FUTURE

THE PARLIAMENTARY CRISIS

The twentieth century has witnessed a widespread decline in the prestige and powers of parliaments throughout the world. At the end of World War I in 1918 a strong, independent parliament, elected by the voters in free elections, with power to check and control the executive officers, was universally regarded as the hallmark of democratic government. By the end of World War II in 1945, however, parliaments were being widely challenged as too slow, as cumbersome political "debating societies," unable to act effectively in coping with the problems of a rapidly changing world. In Communist countries, parliaments existed, if at all, only to ratify the decisions of the ruling group; and, in countries ruled by dictators, parliaments and popular elections have usually been suspended. A leading authority on parliamentary government has declared that "the Congress of the United States is the last effective parliamentary body in any of the great nations."[1]

The loss of confidence in parliament and public cynicism have paved the way for the rise of dictatorships. Following World War I, the parliaments of Germany and Italy were strongly attacked for their inability to cope with widespread unemployment and breakdown of the economic order, leading to the rise of dictators. After World War II, the French parliament was similarly criticized for its inability to govern. The weak French government, frequently turned out of office by a political parliament, was unable, in 1958, to end the insurrection in Algeria, which had dragged along for years. To save the country from civil war and internal revolution, the French parliament recalled Gen. Charles DeGaulle from private life to head the government and voted him the extraordinary powers that he demanded. Subsequently he submitted to the voters a new constitution that created the office of president with near dictatorial powers and sharply curtailed the powers of parliament, which today are only a shadow of its former powers.

The British Parliament, the "Mother of Parliaments," has retained its powers, but today it is virtually run by the Prime Minister, the leader of the majority party in Parliament, and the members of his Cabinet. There is no separation of powers in the British government as in that of the United States. The powers of Parliament are virtually unlimited, but in practice it has delegated most of its functions to the Prime Minister and Cabinet. As in other countries, the powers delegated to the executive have greatly increased in recent decades as the functions of government have vastly increased in size and have become more complex and technical in nature.

The parliaments of other free European countries are similar in many respects to the British Parliament, but multiple-party systems in these countries have resulted in very different parliamentary practices. The parliaments of Canada, Australia, New Zealand, and the other members of the British Commonwealth are patterned after the British

[1] Sir Dennis Brogan, "The Problem of Congress," in *The Congress and America's Future,* Final Report, Occidental College American Assembly, 1964, p. 5.

Parliament. The new nations established since 1945 have usually copied the British Parliament in form; but since they usually operate under a single-party system, their parliaments are ineffective in serving as a check on the executive. Parliaments of countries without experience in democratic government have usually had little power and many have been displaced by virtual dictatorships.

The Congress of the United States, like a few other national legislatures, has retained its independence and power to serve as an effective check on the executive, as was intended by the framers of the Constitution. Through approximately three hundred committees and subcommittees, each provided with a staff, Congress exercises greater control over legislation and administration by the executive departments than the parliaments of other major powers. The real work of Congress is performed by its committees and subcommittees, to which have been delegated large powers. No other national legislature has a comparable committee system. Senior members of Congress, particularly the chairmen of important committees and subcommittees, exert great power not only over legislation within their jurisdiction, but also over the executive departments. An eminent British political scientist wrote in 1940: "The influential members of Congress have, in their legislative capacity, more power than any private members of any other legislative assembly in the world."[2]

THE ROLE OF CONGRESS

EXPANSION OF THE NATIONAL GOVERNMENT During the nineteenth century, when a majority of the American people lived in rural areas and small towns, and agriculture was the dominant industry in most of the country, Congress enacted few laws dealing with social and economic problems. The functions of the national government were limited largely to the conduct of foreign relations, the maintenance of a small defense force, and the administration of the postal system and the federal courts. The philosophy "that government is best which governs least" widely prevailed. Congress passed laws governing the small federal departments, tariffs on imports, excise taxes, public

[2] Harold J. Laski, *The American Presidency: An Interpretation*, Harper & Row, Publishers, Incorporated, New York, 1940, p. 114.

lands, rivers and harbors, and the currency. The cost of the national government was paid largely from tariffs on imports, which in some years provided more funds than the small government departments required. The so-called great debates of Congress dealt with subjects that today appear to be of only minor importance. The legislation passed by Congress ordinarily had little effect on the welfare of the nation; if Congress failed to enact proposed legislation no great harm resulted. Congress had no professional staff to assist it and had little need for one. Members of Congress drafted their own bills, wrote their own speeches, and were able to pass on the simple subjects of legislation without assistance. Special-interest groups, which today are often referred to as the "third house," had relatively little influence on legislation.

The great expansion of the functions and powers of the national government that has taken place during the present century, especially since 1930, has greatly increased the functions and powers of Congress. The great changes in society, including the population explosion, technological revolution, growth of a highly industrialized, urban society, and other developments, have created new problems and needs that require action by the national government. All levels of government have felt the impact of these changes, but the national government has been most affected. Only the national government is able to cope effectively with many of the needs and problems of modern society.

Most of the programs carried on by the national government today were virtually unknown or existed only in rudimentary form in 1900, or even as late as 1930. For example, the national government today spends more than 20 billion dollars annually in support of scientific research, which was virtually nonexistent in the first quarter of the century; it spends annually more than 1.5 billion dollars on medical and health research, or more than the total annual budget in the first decade of the century.

The most important legislation enacted by Congress in recent years deals with subjects that were unknown in 1900 and would not have been regarded as within the powers of Congress if they had been known. Congress enacts legislation today on aviation, space exploration, nuclear power, television, urban renewal, rapid transit, ecology, water and air pollution, social security, welfare, safety in industry and mines, public housing, and many other subjects that were of little or no concern a generation ago.

Because of the great strides in science and technology, the older functions of the national government have vastly increased in size and complexity. In no governmental function is this more marked than in national defense, one of the first and still the largest single function of the government. The gigantic armed services of today, with far-flung establishments around the globe, supersonic airplanes, intercontinental missiles, nuclear-powered submarines with MIRV warheads, early-warning systems, and so on, have become a gigantic organization that relies heavily upon scientific developments to provide defense of the country. One of the great problems of democracies today is how to maintain civilian control of the giant military-industrial complex. Much legislation enacted by Congress today has become so complex and technical in character that only members who have become expert on particular subjects are qualified to form intelligent judgments on the issues involved. As a result, Congress has delegated most decisions to its standing committees and ordinarily accepts their recommendations without change.

The number of employees of the national government has increased 15-fold since 1901, from 351,798 or 1.5 percent of the labor force, to 5,232,819 or 7 percent of the labor force in 1962.[3] Before 1917, the annual budget of the national government was less than 1 billion dollars. The budget submitted to Congress in 1971 totaled more than 229 billion dollars, or approximately one-fourth of the estimated gross national product. It should be noted, however, that state and local government expenditures since the end of World War II have increased almost as rapidly as federal expenditures for civil functions.[4]

Members of Congress often complain that in recent decades it has lost much of its power to the executive. The great expansion of the national government and the huge programs that it administers have

---

[3] Samuel P. Huntington, "Congressional Responses to the Twentieth Century," in David Truman (ed.), *The Congress and America's Future,* Prentice-Hall, Inc., Englewood Cliffs, N.J., 1965, p. 6.

[4] Frederick C. Mosher and Orville F. Poland, *The Costs of American Government,* Dodd, Mead & Company, Inc., New York, 1964, p. 48.

made it necessary for Congress to delegate many decisions to executive officers that it formerly prescribed by statutes. The powers of Congress, however, have not declined but have greatly increased with the expansion of the functions of the national government. At each session, Congress today enacts more important legislation and appropriates more funds than it did in the entire first hundred years of its history; but today it is concerned with policies and goals while formerly it prescribed details of administration. Never before has the task of Congress been as great as it is today. Legislation that it passes affects the lives of all citizens and the economy of the country. Many of its acts today have worldwide effects.

MAJOR FUNCTIONS OF CONGRESS The most important function of Congress is that of passing laws. It shares the legislative power with the President, who recommends policies and legislation and can veto bills passed by Congress. A two-thirds majority of each house is then required to override the veto. The legislative power of Congress is granted by Article I of the Constitution, which provides that it shall have the powers, among others, to lay and collect taxes, to borrow money, to regulate commerce with foreign nations and among the states, to coin money and regulate the value thereof, to create inferior courts, to declare war, to raise and support an army and a navy, and "to make all laws which shall be necessary and proper for carrying into execution the foregoing powers, and all powers vested in the Government of the United States by this Constitution." Several of these powers are extremely broad. Under its power to levy taxes, for example, Congress was able to enact social security legislation that established a national system of old age, survivors', and disability insurance, a state system of unemployment compensation, and other welfare and health programs. Under its power over interstate commerce, Congress is able to regulate wages, hours, conditions of work, and other aspects of management and labor relations, as well as to establish agricultural price-support and crop-control programs that were unknown until recent years. In the words of Justice Benjamin Cardoza, the commerce power of Congress is "as broad as the need that evokes it." Formerly, proposed federal legislation establishing new programs was challenged and debated in Congress on constitutional grounds, but the constitutional issue has been largely resolved by Supreme Court decisions broadly interpreting the powers of Congress.

Under its legislative power, Congress determines the programs that will be carried on by the government, establishes policies, and often prescribes procedures; regulates the armed forces; authorizes foreign-aid programs; fixes the duties on imports and controls our commerce with other countries; controls foreign policies; determines the broad policies for the regulation of transportation, communication, public power, trade practices, and the sale of securities; regulates the use of public lands; provides subsidies for large sectors of the economy; and does a thousand other things.

A second major function of Congress is control of the administration. It creates executive departments, authorizes their activities, fixes their objectives, and regulates their operations. Through the power to appropriate funds for the support of government, Congress exercises one of its most potent controls over the executive departments. Before funds are voted, the appropriations committees review in considerable detail not only the department estimates but their work plans, administration, and past performance. Many directions, both official and unofficial, are given to the departments by the appropriations committees. All standing legislative committees are directed by the Legislative Reorganization Act of 1946 to exercise continuous oversight of the departments within their purview.

A third function of Congress is to conduct investigations, not only of the administration of the executive departments, but also into social and economic problems. Investigations are essential to provide Congress with the information and knowledge that it requires to legislate wisely on the multitude of public issues. Investigations are also used to inform the public, to build up public support for or opposition to government policies. They have often been used primarily to secure party or factional advantage, or to publicize an ambitious chairman. At times the investigative function has appeared to overshadow the other functions of Congress.

Another function of Congress is to educate and inform the public. Woodrow Wilson wrote:

It is the proper duty of a representative body to look diligently into every affair of government and to talk much about what it sees. It is meant to be the eyes and the voice, and to embody the wisdom and will of its constituents. ... The informing function of Congress should be preferred even to its legislative function.[5]

The same point of view was expressed by John Stuart Mill:

I know not how a representative assembly can more usefully employ itself than in talk, when the subject of talk is the great public interests of the country, and every sentence of it represents the opinion either of some important body of persons in the nation, or an individual in whom some such body have reposed their confidence.[6]

The informing function is performed today largely through committee hearings on important legislative proposals and through congressional investigations. Debate on the floor of each house has become largely a lost art, especially in the House of Representatives, which places severe limitations on the time allotted for debate. Although the level of debate in the Senate is higher, it is the proceedings of the major committees rather than the floor debates that attract greatest attention.

Another major function of Congress is to propose amendments to the Constitution and to specify whether ratification by the states shall be by votes of the state legislatures or by conventions. Constitutional amendments must be passed by a two-thirds vote in each house, and must be approved by three-fourths of the states. The Constitution also provides that on application of two-thirds of the state legislatures, Congress shall call a constitutional convention to propose amendments, a method that has not been used. Significantly, no provision is made for a popular vote on constitutional amendments, which is required by all of the states for approval of state constitutional amendments.

Although numerous amendments are proposed at each session of Congress, few are adopted. The most important changes have been accomplished by interpretation of the meaning of the Constitution by

[5]Woodrow Wilson, *Congressional Government*, Houghton Mifflin Company, Boston, 1885, p. 303.
[6]*On Liberty and Representative Government*, Oxford University Press, Fair Lawn, N.J., 1948, p. 175.

the Supreme Court rather than by formal amendment. The broad grant of powers to the federal government in the Constitution has permitted its growth through judicial interpretation to meet the changing needs of the country.

OTHER FUNCTIONS Congress performs a variety of other functions. Each house determines its own rules and procedures. It meets in joint session every four years to count the electoral votes, and in the event that no candidate for President receives a majority, the House of Representatives elects a President from the highest three candidates, each state casting one vote.

Under the Constitution, each house is the "Judge of the Elections, Returns, and Qualifications of its own Members." When elections are contested, each house assigns the contest to a committee, which conducts an inquiry and reports its recommendation to the parent house. Formerly, election frauds, bribery, and irregularities in elections were often charged; and numerous contests came before the House of Representatives, but fortunately the contests today are relatively few.

In passing on the qualifications of members, as provided in the Constitution, each house has denied admission, on various grounds, to persons certified as duly elected; but, as we shall see, a decision of the United States Supreme Court in 1969 severely limits the power of each house to exclude persons who have been certified as duly elected. The House of Representatives once excluded Victor Berger, the Socialist candidate who was elected from a Milwaukee district but later admitted him to take his seat after the voters of his district reelected him by a large majority. Two Utah citizens were denied admission on the ground that they had practiced polygamy, and a former member of the House was excluded because he had been found guilty of selling appointments to the military academy.[7]

Before 1913, the Senate excluded a number of persons elected to the Senate by state legislatures on a finding that fraud and bribery had been used in the election. Several persons popularly elected to the Senate in the 1920s were excluded because of excessive cam-

[7] George B. Galloway, *History of the House of Representatives,* Thomas Y. Crowell Company, New York, 1961, pp. 31–32.

paign expenditures.[8] Huge campaign expenditures on behalf of candidates for the Senate have since been common, particularly in the larger states, but no exclusions on this ground have been made in recent years.

In a case that attracted nationwide attention in 1967, the House refused to seat Adam Clayton Powell, a Negro congressman from New York City, who had served in Congress for many years and for a number of terms as chairman of the House Committee on Education and Labor. He was charged in the press with flagrant misuse of committee funds for pleasure trips abroad for himself and members of his staff and for placing his wife, who resided in Puerto Rico, on the payroll and collecting her salary. Powell's junketing and high living at public expense were widely reported in the press and raised a storm of public indignation. He made no attempt to deny or to explain his spending of public funds for personal use but maintained that other members had done the same and threatened to expose them if he was denied his seat. His offense was not merely that he had junketed at public expense, which is commonly done by members of Congress, or even his improper use of committee funds, but rather that he did so openly and brazenly, bringing discredit on the House. Members were flooded with letters from constituents demanding that Powell be denied his seat.

The Democratic caucus, which met before the opening of Congress, stripped him of his seniority and chairmanship; and the House subsequently refused to permit him to take his seat. Charging that he had been excluded because of his race, Powell instituted court action to force the House to seat him. Before his case reached the Supreme Court, his district reelected him by a large majority, but the House again refused to seat him.

The Supreme Court ruled that the House cannot add to the qualifications prescribed in the Constitution; namely, a member must be 25 years of age, a citizen of the United States for seven years, and an inhabitant of the state from which he is elected.[9] After Powell agreed to deductions from his salary to reimburse the government for funds

[8] George H. Haynes, *The Senate of the United States,* Houghton Mifflin Company, Boston, 1938, vol. I, chap. 4.

[9] *Powell v. McCormack,* 23 U.S. Supreme Court Reports 491, June 16, 1969.

improperly spent by him, the House permitted him to take his seat, but he lost his seniority and chairmanship. Two years later, he was defeated for reelection by another candidate of his race.

CENSURE OF MEMBERS   Each house may discipline its members and by a two-thirds majority may expel a member for any reasons it sees fit. The power of expulsion has rarely been used except during the Civil War, when a number of Southern members were expelled for treason. A few members have resigned after charges were brought against them.

Each house is extremely tolerant of the conduct of its members. In only a few instances have members been officially censured. A few members have been convicted of serious crimes while in office without being censured. The most sensational recent censure was that of Sen. Joseph McCarthy of Wisconsin in 1954. In the early 1950s, Senator McCarthy shocked the country by sensational charges that the State Department had been infiltrated by Communists. These charges, which were never supported by credible evidence, inflamed public opinion at a time when the relations between this country and the Soviets were severely strained and led to the institution of loyalty investigations throughout the federal service.

In 1953, Senator McCarthy became chairman of the Senate Permanent Investigation Subcommittee and secured a large appropriation for a staff to conduct investigations and to hold hearings to expose alleged Communist infiltration of the federal service. Witnesses who were subpoenaed to testify, usually in closed hearings with only the Senator from Wisconsin and staff present (other members of the subcommittee soon refused to participate in the hearings), were browbeaten, denied their constitutional rights, and were usually smeared as Communists or Communist sympathizers in statements to the press by the Senator following the hearings. Witnesses had no means of defending themselves, and some lost their jobs and were unable to find other employment because of the accusations made against them.

The attacks made by Senator McCarthy on members of the State Department, including Foreign Service officers with distinguished careers, demoralized the Department at a critical period in the conduct of foreign affairs. In an attempt to appease the Senator from Wisconsin, Secretary of State John Foster Dulles appointed, with unfortunate results, a person formerly associated with the Senator to head the sensitive Security Division. At one time, it was reported that Senator McCarthy had as much control over the Department as did the Secretary of State. Columnist Walter Lippmann declared that, unless Senator McCarthy was curbed in his drive for power through his investigations, the constitutional balance of power between the legislative and executive branches would be seriously altered.

Senator McCarthy next turned his investigations on the Department of the Army and opened hearings on alleged Communist infiltration of Army personnel at Fort Monmouth, a technical facility. The Army fought back and, insisting on open hearings, engaged a distinguished jurist, Joseph Welch of Boston, as chief counsel. The hearings, which were televised, attracted a nationwide audience overnight and were watched by millions. Senator McCarthy met his match in Mr. Welch, whose quiet manner, unfailing courtesy, and keen wit contrasted with the blustering tactics and browbeating of witnesses by the Senator from Wisconsin. The hearings were soon suspended amid an uproar by the press and public. A year later when the Army completed its careful investigation of charges against the Fort Monmouth personnel, it found no disloyal persons among its employees and reinstated those who had been suspended.

The downfall of the Senator came when he turned his attacks on members of the Senate who had dared to criticize his actions. At the height of his power, few members of the Senate had dared to oppose his actions publicly. Charges were filed against him by a group of senators; and, following extended hearings and debate, the Senate voted to censure him for conduct unbecoming a senator. The wording of the resolution was restrained, but it destroyed his power and ended his political career.

In 1969, the Senate censured Sen. Thomas Dodd of Connecticut for failing to report campaign contributions which he had devoted to personal use as income and for other financial irregularities and unethical conduct. Senator Dodd denied that he was guilty of any illegal or improper conduct and retained his office until the end of his term, but he failed to secure the support or nomination of his party in 1970, and was defeated in his bid for reelection as an independent.

The House of Representatives has the power to impeach civil officers of the United States, including the President, who thereupon are tried by the Senate, acting as a judicial body. A two-thirds vote of the Senate is required to convict an officer on impeachment charges. Although the framers of the Constitution anticipated that this procedure would provide the means of removing officers who were guilty of misconduct or abuse of their trust, the power has seldom been used.

Each house may punish a private person for conduct that interferes with its work and for contempt (as failure to answer questions put to him by an investigating committee) by ordering the Sergeant at Arms to hold him in custody. Such punishment, however, is limited to the period that Congress is in session. When Congress adjourns, a person so incarcerated must be released. Congress follows the practice today of turning over recalcitrant witnesses who are cited for contempt to the Justice Department for prosecution.

Congress admits new states to the Union. Each house determines its own rules, except those provided in the Constitution itself. The Senate alone is granted the power to advise and consent to treaties and to approve or disapprove presidential nominations to most offices, civil and military. The requirement that treaties must be approved by a two-thirds vote of the Senate has given it preeminence over the House in foreign affairs, though legislation and appropriations to implement such treaties require the approval of both houses.

Although the powers granted to Congress are great, they are not unlimited. Bills that it passes and joint resolutions having the effect of law require the signature of the President, unless they are passed by a two-thirds majority by both houses over the President's veto. Acts of Congress are also subject to review by the courts and may be overruled on the ground that they are not within the powers granted to the federal government by the Constitution or that they violate some constitutional provision. The Supreme Court determines the meaning of provisions of the Constitution and whether statutes passed by Congress, as well as the actions of executive officers, are constitutional.

THE ADOPTION OF A BICAMERAL LEGISLATURE

The decision of the framers of the Constitution to establish a bicameral legislative body consisting of the House of Representatives and the Senate was one of the "great compromises" of the Convention. The smaller states, fearing that a single legislative body apportioned among the states on the basis of population would lead to its domination by a few of the larger states, were able to secure the creation of a second chamber in which each state, regardless of population, would have equal representation. The fears of the smaller states proved to be groundless; there has seldom, if ever, been a division in the House of Representatives in which the more populous states were aligned on one side against the smaller states. But the system of representation that gives all states equal representation in the Senate is firmly established in the Constitution and cannot be changed without the consent of every state.

The framers of the Constitution feared that the lower house, being directly elected by the people and responsive to their demands, would be moved by popular passions and act hastily, violating the rights of property owners and the well-to-do. It was thought that the Senate, being a smaller body and composed of older persons selected by the state legislatures, would provide a check on radical legislation passed by the lower house. For the first hundred years, the Senate was, indeed, the more conservative body, and, being composed largely of men of wealth, was called the "millionaires' club." Since the adoption in 1913 of the Seventeenth Amendment, which provided for popular election of senators, the Senate has often been more liberal than the House of Representatives.

MOVEMENT FOR CONGRESSIONAL REFORM

As World War II came to an end in 1945, there was widespread recognition that Congress needed to be strengthened and reformed to equip it to deal with the emerging problems of the postwar period. During the war and the crisis years of the Great Depression of the 1930s, Congress had delegated unprecedented emergency powers to the President and the executive departments, and many felt that the time had come for Congress to reassert its powers and regain its position as a coordinate branch of the government. It was foreseen that during the postwar period Congress would be called upon to determine policies and programs of far greater importance and complexity than it had formerly passed upon. The United States was looked to by its allies to provide leadership in developing international organizations to maintain the peace, to provide the major part of the assistance needed to rebuild the war-ravaged countries, and to aid underdeveloped emerging nations. To deal wisely and promptly with problems as they developed, Congress needed better organization and staffing, together with new rules and procedures that would enable it to act without undue delays.

In 1945, Congress created a Joint Committee on the Organization of Congress to inquire into its operations and to recommend improvements. After conducting lengthy hearings, in 1946, the joint committee submitted its report, in which it recommended numerous changes in the organization and functioning of Congress. Many of these recommendations were enacted in the Legislative Reorganization Act of 1946. The senate report on the act stated:

> Devised to handle the simpler tasks of an earlier day, our legislative machinery and procedures are by common consent no longer competent to cope satisfactorily with the grave and complex problems of the post-war world. They must be modernized if we are to avoid an imminent breakdown of the legislative branch of the national government.[10]

The Legislative Reorganization Act of 1946 included the following major provisions: (1) The number of standing committees of the Senate was reduced from 33 to 15, and of the House from 48 to 19. (2) The standing committees were provided with professionally trained staffs with higher salaries to attract qualified persons. (3) Each standing committee was authorized to conduct investigations and directed to exercise oversight of departments and agencies within its jurisdictions. (4) The salaries of members of Congress were increased, larger allowances were provided for staff assistance, and a retirement system was established for members of Congress.

The most important reform accomplished by the act was to increase and strengthen the staffs of Congress, which has greatly facilitated the work of the standing committees and of individual members. The reduction in the number of standing committees proved to be illusory because of the greatly increased use of subcommittees, which today

[10] Report 1400, 79th Cong., 2nd Sess., p. 2.

number more than 250. It is not unusual for standing committees to have from 10 to 15 subcommittees, many of which function very much as independent committees.

Although the Legislative Reorganization Act of 1946 was hailed as a great reform, within a few years it was recognized that in fact it had made little change in the operation of Congress and had not corrected defects in its rules and procedures that often render it ineffective. The resolution creating the joint committee that prepared the act prohibited it from recommending any change "with reference to the rules, parliamentary practices, and/or precedents of either House," a provision indicating that the congressional leaders were opposed to any real reform. The joint committee was thus prohibited from recommending any change in the unwritten rule of seniority, which had long been criticized. It was also prohibited from proposing any change in the rule of unlimited debate in the Senate or the power of the Rules Committee of the House to block consideration of legislation that a majority of its members opposed. The dispersion of power over legislation to more than three hundred committees and subcommittees, particularly to the chairmen of committees who owe their positions to the automatic rule of seniority, remained unchanged. The Reorganization Act of 1946 strengthened the committees as centers of power, which continue to operate as "little legislatures," subject to little or no control or responsibility.

RECENT CRITICISM OF CONGRESS   In his first State of the Union address to Congress in 1961, President John F. Kennedy said: "Before my term is ended we shall have to test anew whether a nation organized and governed as ours can endure. The outcome is by no means certain." The first test came at the outset of his term. Unless it could be changed, the powerful Rules Committee of the House, controlled by a coalition of two conservative Southern Democrats and four conservative Northern Republicans, headed by 78-year-old Howard Smith of Virginia, one of the most conservative members of Congress, would undoubtedly block consideration by the House of most of President Kennedy's legislative program. Speaker Sam Rayburn undertook to curb the conservative control of the committee and won a narrow victory, adding three members to the Committee, two of whom were liberal Democrats. President Kennedy was thus able to secure consideration of his legislative program. Despite the large Democratic majority in each house, Congress failed to act on most of his important bills, including Medicare, aid to education, public housing, foreign trade, reduction of the income tax, and creation of a department of urban affairs. Speaking in New York in 1962, he said: "When I was a Congressman I never realized how important Congress is, but now I do."[11]

What happened to President Kennedy's progressive legislative program was accurately described by James Reston, head of *The New York Times* Washington Bureau, who wrote:

> The President will go to the Hill and define the State of the Union in iambic pentameter. ... Then after partisan applause of the soaring phrases ... the Chinese Bandits will take over. The vast panorama of the nation in the world will be cut up into little pieces, each committee chairman will vanish into his privileged sanctuary with his special part of the picture and the vast decentralized Congressional machine will begin to grind. ... Congress operates not as a unified institution but as a loose confederation of virtually autonomous committees headed by a handful of immensely powerful and often capricious chairmen. Thus the function of Congress is scattered among the chairmen of almost 300 committees and subcommittees whose activities are seldom coordinated and whose action in the end militates against a coherent legislative program.[12]

The trouble wrote Reston, is not the congressmen, most of whom are conscientious and industrious, with ethical standards as high as leaders of the executive, "but all are caught up in a system which most of them criticize but none can change."

In the aftermath of the assassination of President Kennedy in November, 1963, President Lyndon B. Johnson, a past master of parliamentary maneuver, who had been the strongest majority leader in the history of the Senate, succeeded in securing the passage of much of Kennedy's legislative program in 1964 and more in 1965, during the honeymoon period after his election as President by an overwhelming majority. Criticism of Congress for its inability to legislate and its ineffec-

---

[11] Quoted by Tom Wicker, *New York Times*, Dec. 26, 1970.
[12] *New York Times*, Jan. 7, 1963.

tiveness declined, but its critics maintained that its basic weaknesses remained. In his last two years in office, President Johnson lost his magic touch and had increasing difficulty in securing enactment of his legislative recommendations.

On entering office in 1969, President Richard M. Nixon was confronted with a Congress both houses of which were controlled by the Democrats. He recommended little legislation in his first year in office, and Congress passed only a few of the bills he recommended in 1970. When Congress recessed for the Christmas holidays in 1970, the Senate had been tied up with several concurrent filibusters and threatened filibusters and had not passed a number of the major legislative recommendations of the President, including family assistance; supersonic transport; import quotas on textiles, shoes, and other goods; aid to school districts undergoing integration, federal sharing of revenue with states and cities, and increased social security payments. In an interview, the President declared that the Ninety-first Congress would be remembered "not for what it did, but for what it failed to do. . . . In the final months and weeks of 1970 . . . the nation was presented with a spectacle of a legislative body, especially the Senate, that had seemingly lost the capacity to decide and the will to act."[13] The conservative *Wall Street Journal,* however, defended Congress for its failure to pass the bills on family assistance, supersonic transport, and import quotas, stating that the bills were controversial and of dubious benefits to the nation and that further consideration was needed. "At times, after all," stated the editorial, "there are positive virtues in legislative inaction."[14] At the opening of the new Congress in 1971, President Nixon resubmitted 40 measures that had failed to pass during the preceding session.

Much of the criticism of Congress in recent years is concerned with its inability to enact without long delays needed legislation dealing with the urgent problems of the nation. In most years, Congress adjourns after a long session without taking action on many of the pressing problems before it. Because of its dilatory procedures, it has failed in recent years to pass some appropriations until months after

[13] *San Francisco Chronicle,* Jan. 6, 1971.
[14] Jan. 5, 1971.

the start of the fiscal year to which they apply, seriously handicapping orderly administration. At every session, it passes many minor and uncontroversial measures, and in serious emergencies it can act promptly; but often it is unable to enact legislation dealing with urgent problems until they reach crisis proportions.

Despite the rapid increase in crime and statistics showing the high percentage of violent crimes committed by armed criminals, the gun lobby has been able for years to prevent national legislation regulating firearms. For many years, the pure food and drug legislation was pitifully weak; and only after the sensational news broke of the tragic effects of thalidomide on unborn infants was it possible to get Congress to pass legislation mildly strengthening the law. Disastrous oil spills have continued to occur in recent years without any action by Congress to pass needed regulations to protect the public and our environment. Mining disasters continue to occur, taking the lives of hundreds of miners without bringing needed federal action. Reformers have warned for years of the urgent need for reform of the electoral college, but Congress has taken no action. Excessive campaign expenditures have long been a serious threat to democratic government, but Congress has not taken any effective action. President Theodore Roosevelt urged sweeping legislation on campaign expenditures in 1907, but 65 years later federal regulation is, in President Johnson's words, "more loophole than law." These are only a few of the many examples that could be given of the failure of Congress to enact legislation when it is needed.

It is essential that Congress be able to consider and determine policies and enact legislation on the urgent problems of society within a reasonable amount of time, but it is equally important that it not legislate until it has given adequate consideration to proposed legislation. Action without debate is folly, but debate without action renders the legislature impotent and contemptible. Delay is wise if the legislation is controversial and additional time is required to educate the public, to compromise different points of view, and to win acceptance, even though reluctant, of interest groups that are primarily concerned. In a much-quoted passage in *The Federalist* (No. 10), James Madison wisely observed that in all civilized nations there will necessarily be many factions or interests, "a landed interest, a manufacturing interest, a mercantile interest, with many lesser interests. . . . The regulation of these various and interfering interests forms the principal task of modern legislation."

The framers of the Constitution did not favor a legislative body that would act hastily but on the contrary provided checks and balances to safeguard against hasty action. Two houses of Congress were provided, each of which must approve legislation. In addition, the President was given a qualified veto of acts passed by the two houses of Congress as an additional safeguard against ill-considered legislation. The members of the Constitutional Convention were well acquainted with the manipulation and ill-considered legislation of the state legislatures elected by the people, and they created the Senate whose members were to be chosen by the state legislatures from the well-to-do men of affairs to serve as a check on the popularly elected chamber. In their day, little national legislation was needed, and their prime concern was to provide safeguards against unwise legislation.

The needs of the nation today, however, nearly two hundred years later, are fundamentally different from those that existed when Congress first met. National legislation today affects the lives of all citizens and deals with almost all aspects of the economy and society. An effective Congress, truly representative of the people and responsive to their needs, able to legislate wisely and without undue delay on a multitude of problems, is needed if this nation is to endure.[15]

In 1970, the prestigious Committee for Economic Development, which consists of the chief executive officers of many of the largest corporations in the country, issued *Making Congress More Effective,* a report that urged numerous specific reforms to modernize congressional procedures and make Congress more effective. On the need for congressional reform the report stated:

This country is in the throes of change. Congress, like every institution must respond to transformation wrought by science, technology, and education upon every aspect of urban and rural life. Business concerns of all

[15] See David B. Truman (ed.), *The Congress and America's Future,* Prentice-Hall, Inc., Englewood Cliffs, N.J., 1965. This series of essays was sponsored by the American Assembly of Columbia University. Parallel conferences on Congress and America's Future were held at a number of leading universities in 1964 and 1965.

kinds, universities, even religious organizations and the family are subject to continuous modification. There is now a rising insistence that government must adapt itself to deal more effectively with new and challenging conditions.

As its burdens have grown in range and scope far beyond anything foreseen only a few years ago, a competent and vital Congress is more essential than ever before. The formulation of public policy is a joint responsibility shared with the Executive Branch, but in the final analysis it is Congress that adopts (or rejects) legislation that determines the health of the economy, the national security, the character of life both urban and rural, the condition of the environment, and the levels of generational, racial and other group tensions. The people of the country have every right to insist upon a responsive and effective Congress.[16]

THE CONGRESSIONAL REORGANIZATION ACT OF 1970 In 1963, a group of 32 Senators of both political parties introduced a concurrent resolution (a concurrent resolution requires approval by both houses) at the opening of Congress to create a joint committee to study the organization and operation of Congress and to recommend needed improvements. The proposed joint committee was patterned after the 1945 Joint Committee on the Organization of Congress, but its terms of reference were broader. Before reporting the resolution to the Senate nine months later, the Rules Committee, over the strong objections of Democratic Sen. Joseph S. Clark and Republican Sen. Hugh Scott of Pennsylvania, amended the resolution to prohibit the proposed joint committee from making any recommendation relating to the rules, parliamentary procedures, or precedents of either house. The two Pennsylvania Senators declared that this provision defeated the very purpose of creating a joint committee to recommend improvements in the organization and operation of Congress.

The concurrent resolution was passed by the Senate, but in the House it was referred to the Rules Committee where it was buried because of the opposition of the Speaker and powerful committee chairmen. Two years later, in 1965, the Senate repassed the resolution and by this time the demand for congressional reform in the

[16] Pages 9–10.

House, particularly by younger members, was strong and the resolution was adopted.

In May, 1965, the Joint Committee on the Organization of Congress, consisting of five members from each house, began extended hearings, which were subsequently published in 15 volumes. The Joint Committee *Report* issued in 1966 stated: It is becoming more and more difficult for Congress to meet its responsibilities [in] . . . an increasingly complex society [which] produces social, economic, and technological problems of staggering complexity. Many contend that Congress is no longer capable of exercising initiative in the solution of modern problems." The reason for the loss of initiative by Congress and the increasing delegation to the executive branch was attributed to the lack of "organizational effectiveness" by Congress.[17] The Committee made more than a hundred recommendations to make Congress more effective.

Most recommendations of the committee called for minor changes in the rules and procedures of each house and its committees. No major change was proposed. Senator A. S. Mike Monroney of Oklahoma, Democràtic cochairman of the joint committee, declared that the bill to carry out the recommendations did not contain "a single spectacular thing."[18] No recommendation was made for modification of the seniority rule (which was held to be purely a party matter), of the power of the House Rules Committee to block consideration of bills that a majority of its members opposed, or of the filibuster in the Senate, which is used to prevent the Senate from acting on pending legislation. The changes proposed in the bill to bring about improved procedures were largely noncontroversial; they were also relatively unimportant. Most of the significant changes were toned down by amendments adopted in the House and Senate. One significant change was that standing committees shall report by names the *roll-call* votes of members on bills and amendments. Intended to remove the veil of secrecy that has historically shrouded the actions of committees, it will be effective only to the extent that roll-call votes are taken in committees. It is probably safe to say that it is unlikely to

---

[17] *Organization of Congress, Final Report,* 89th Cong., 2d Sess. Senate Report no. 1414, July 28, 1966, p. 1.

[18] Lyn Shepard, *Christian Science Monitor,* Jan. 28, 1967.

achieve the intended result. Another significant change was to provide that one-fifth of a quorum in the House of Representatives may require that a record shall be made of how each member voted on an amendment when a teller vote is taken. This amendment was intended to remove the secrecy about how each member votes on amendments when the House is sitting as a committee of the whole.

The Congressional Reorganization Act of 1970 (its official name) authorized the broadcasting of committee hearings in the House (such broadcasts were already permitted in the Senate), prohibited proxy voting in committee (if the committee so decided), and created a permanent Joint Committee on Congressional Operations. The professional staff authorized for each standing committee was increased from four to six persons, two of whom were to be assigned to serve the minority party members of the committee if so requested. It should be noted that with the exception of two or three standing committees, all committees already had far larger staffs, which have been authorized by each house. Several committee staffs exceed 100 persons. The only effect of the provision was to authorize the assignment of professional staff to serve minority members. Whether it is wise for each committee to have two separate staffs, one Democratic and the other Republican, is debatable.

The provisions of the act relating to rules and procedures of each house and its committees have no binding effect since each house is authorized by the Constitution to determine its own rules and may amend, disregard, or revise the provisions of the act. The provisions relating to the procedures of standing committees are hortatory, and as such may have some effect, but this is problematical. They attempt to state what is good practice, and in most cases the procedure recommended is already being followed by some committees. Most committees have adopted rules and procedures, which they are free to alter or disregard. It has been said that there is no power on earth that can force a committee of Congress to observe its rules.

Congress took seven years and ten months to enact a modest reform act, which it is doubtful will have much effect on its operations. During the debate on the bill, Senator Clark of Pennsylvania, a leading advocate of congressional reform, declared: "The fact of the matter is that Congress does not want to reform itself." As a French maxim goes: "The more it is changed, the more it is the same."

PROSPECT What is the prospect for congressional reform? What reforms are needed to make Congress more effective, more responsive to public needs, to enable it to enact needed legislation without long delays, and to serve as an effective check on the executive? Most political scientists and political writers are convinced that Congress will be slow in adopting reforms, particularly major reforms that would threaten the power structure. Some political scientists maintain that Congress is unable to reform itself and that as a consequence the trend to delegate greater powers to the executive will continue.[19] An outstanding writer on Congress, Ralph K. Huitt, contends that it is unrealistic to expect Congress to reform itself, which would mean that power would be taken from those who hold it and placed in other hands. He defends the present dispersion of power and responsibility in Congress:

> There is a case . . . to be made for the dispersal of power in Congress. It has the strengths of the free enterprise system: it multiplies the decision makers, the points of access to influence and power, and the creative moving agents. It is hard to believe that a small group of leaders would do better. What is gained in orderliness might be lost in vitality and sensitiveness to pressures for change.[20]

Congress is a conservative institution with regard to its own organization and procedures; its rules, practices, and traditions have developed over many years and they are not about to be changed in a hurry. Those who hold positions of great power and prestige rarely look with favor on changes that would weaken that power or might place it in other hands. The power structure of the House and Senate—the senior members who are chairmen or high-ranking members of the major committees and the party leaders—with few exceptions are wedded to the traditions and methods of Congress in which they have acquired power; and they see no reason for change. Senior members invariably support the rule of seniority and regard colleagues who criticize it as disloyal. Institutional loyalty is expected of those who wish to become a part of the ruling establishment. The late Sen.

[19] See James M. Burns, *Congress on Trial,* Harper & Row, Publishers, Incorporated, New York, 1949, *passim.*
[20] Commission on Money and Credit, *Fiscal Debt Management Policies,* Prentice-Hall, Inc., Englewood Cliffs, N.J., 1963, p. 494.

Everett Dirksen of Illinois, Senate Republican leader, defended the Senate against criticisms for delay in passing needed legislation: "The Senate is much like an old scow. It does not move fast; it does not move very far at one time; but it does not sink."[21]

The support in Congress for congressional reform comes principally from junior members who are frustrated because the existing rules and traditions place great power in the hands of a relatively few senior members and prevent junior members from taking any meaningful and satisfying part in the work of Congress until they have acquired seniority.[22] In the past, junior members have usually been reluctant to criticize Congress, knowing that to do so would incur the displeasure of the establishment, and have bided their time, hoping by continuous reelection over a period of years to achieve seniority and advance to positions of power and prestige. In recent years, however, a group of impatient younger members of both parties in the House have boldly pressed for reforms.

Changes in the organization and procedures of Congress will not come quickly but will take place slowly when the need is clear and the change can no longer be postponed. The Senate has modified slightly the cloture rule to stop filibusters; every new Senator today is assured of receiving one "good" committee assignment of his choice, although formerly he had to wait. On several occasions, the House has for one session curbed the power of the Rules Committee to block consideration of pending legislation. Congress has greatly improved its professional staff since 1945. Like all other human institutions it must change if it is to survive.

Greater cooperation between Congress and the President is required if either branch is to be effective, but competition, opposition, and distrust often prevail instead of mutual respect and cooperation.

---

[21] Quoted by Joseph S. Clark, *Congress: The Sapless Branch,* Harper & Row, Publishers, Incorporated, New York, 1965, p. 129.

[22] The complaint of the new congressman was graphically stated by Everett G. Burkholder, Democratic representative from California, in announcing in 1964 that he would not be a candidate for reelection. "I could see that I wasn't going to get any place. Nobody listens to what you have to say until you've been here 10 or 12 years. These old men have got everything so tied down you can't do anything. There are only about 40 of the 435 members who call the shots. They're the committee chairmen and ranking members and they're all around 70 or 80." *The Washington Post,* April 3, 1964.

The Constitution provides for separate branches of government, but it does not require that they be opponents. A weakness of the Constitution is that it permits and invites divided control. In 10 of the 12 years between 1952 and 1972 when Republican Presidents were in office, the Democratic party controlled both houses of Congress. Democratic Presidents did not fare much better, for they were usually opposed in Congress by a coalition of conservative Republicans from the North and West and Southern conservative Democrats. This constitutional defect would be lessened if members of the House served four years and were elected in the same year as the President.

The need for improvement of congressional control of the budget and finance has long been recognized, but Congress is slow to change outmoded practices. This subject is discussed in a later chapter. More able and promising candidates would stand for the House of Representatives if membership were a stepping stone to advancement to higher office, as it is in the British House of Commons. In recent years, the Senate has become the stepping stone for presidential candidates, who formerly were selected largely from the governors of the leading states.

The purpose of this review of the movement for congressional reform in recent years is to introduce the student to the study of Congress. An awareness of the criticisms of Congress and the proposals for reform will add much to the significance of the subsequent chapters. The role of the member of Congress, how he is recruited and elected, his relations with constituents, and his participation in the legislative process are discussed in the following chapter. The committee system, procedures in each house, the power of committee chairmen, the rule of seniority, party leadership, Congress and the President, the Speaker, the House Rules Committee, filibusters, and congressional control of administration and finance are discussed in the following chapters.

REVIEW QUESTIONS

1. What have been the principal causes of the crisis of parliaments throughout the free world during the past half century?

2. Compare the activities of Congress today with those of 1900 with regard to each of the following: international affairs, national defense, welfare, education, civil rights, science and technology, and control of the executive departments.

3. Comment on Mill's statement: "I know not how a representative assembly can more usefully employ itself than in talk," with reference to quality of debate and discussion in each house of Congress.

4. Why were the changes adopted in the 1946 Legislative Reorganization Act ineffective in improving the operations of Congress?

5. Describe in some detail the various functions performed by Congress in passing legislation, controlling administration, and the like.

6. What are the powers of Congress to pass on the qualifications of persons duly elected to Congress? Comment on the Adam Clayton Powell case. Do you agree with the decisions of the Supreme Court in the case? Explain. What use has each house made of its power to censure members?

7. Why did the late President Kennedy face so much trouble in securing congressional approval of his legislative proposals?

8. Write an essay on the need for a more effective Congress, stating the reforms that you consider to be most important and why.

9. What were the more important changes made by the Legislative Reorganization Act of 1970?

2 THE MEMBER OF CONGRESS AND HIS WORLD

THE CONGRESSMEN

PRESTIGE After witnessing a session of the House of Representatives in 1831, a distinguished French visitor, Alexis de Tocqueville, wrote that "one is struck by the vulgar demeanors of that great assembly. Often there is not a distinguished man in the whole number. Its members are almost all obscure individuals . . . mostly village lawyers, men in trade, or even persons of the lower classes of society."[1] Much more favorably impressed by the Senate, which then was elected by the state legislatures, he wrote: "The Senate is com-

---

[1] *Democracy in America*, Alfred A. Knopf, Inc., New York, 1945, vol. 1, p. 204.

posed of eloquent advocates, distinguished generals, and statesmen of note, whose language would at all times do honor to the most remarkable parliamentary debates of Europe." If a de Tocqueville could visit Congress today, nearly 150 years later, he would form a very different opinion of the qualifications of its members. He would doubtless be impressed by the high level of ability, education, and stature of the members of both houses, especially the Senate, which attracts the political leaders of the country. He would certainly be impressed by the two large, luxurious Senate office buildings, the large office staff that each senator has, as well as the three large office buildings occupied by the members of the House. No European parliament can boast of similar quarters and staff.

The Senate no longer includes retired generals among its members, but a few senators hold reserve commissions, a practice that has been criticized. Many senators are former governors of states, others have served several terms in the House of Representatives before being elected to the Senate; a few have served as members of the President's Cabinet. Almost all have had previous public experience. Membership in the Senate is widely regarded as the highest elective public office in the nation except President and Vice President. Senators enjoy great prestige, power, and the opportunity to render distinguished public service.

The Senate has been called the "most exclusive club in the world." Formerly, when its members were elected by the state legislatures, they included many men of great wealth and the Senate was often referred to as the "millionaires' club." The framers of the Constitution thought the Senate ought to represent the wealth of the country in order to serve as a check on the popularly elected House of Representatives. Their expectations were realized in the early history of the Senate. "The Senate roll during the period from 1789 to 1801," writes Roy Swanstrom in a study of the early history of the Senate, "sounded like a 'Who's Who' of the wealthy and prominent of the day."[2] All parts of the country sent men of wealth to the Senate. Robert Morris and William Bingham of Pennsylvania were among the wealthiest men in the country and entertained on a lavish scale, far

---

[2] *The United States Senate: 1787–1801*, U.S. Government Printing Office, 1962, pp. 42–43.

beyond that of the President. Their wives were social leaders. Charles Carroll of Maryland was reputed to be the richest man in America. Even John Taylor of Virginia, spokesman of the Jeffersonian liberals, was a wealthy plantation owner.

Today only a few senators are wealthy, but many are persons of national recognition. The Senate is a way of life for its members. Wherever they go they are treated with great deference. When leading senators speak on important national issues, what they say is reported not only in the press of their own state but throughout the nation and even abroad. For most senators, service in the Senate is the pinnacle of a distinguished political career.

Approximately two-thirds of the members of the House of Representatives have held other public office before their election; one-fourth have served as members of state legislatures and more than 40 percent have held other state or local offices. One-third of the members have not had previous public experience, but a large majority of these have been active in their party organization and most have been prominent in civic affairs.[3] A considerable number of members are under 40 years of age when first elected to the House; few have held high public office or have achieved prominence outside their own congressional districts.

CAREER OPPORTUNITIES   Formerly, many members of Congress were appointed to the President's Cabinet. Huntington reports that from 1861 to 1896, 37 percent of the members of the Cabinet were former members of Congress.[4] The number declined to 19 percent from 1897 to 1940, and has since declined further. No senator has been appointed to the Cabinet since 1952. Representative Stewart Udall served as Secretary of Interior in the Cabinet under Presidents Kennedy and Johnson, and Rep. Melvin Laird served as Secretary of Defense under President Nixon. Senators are no longer willing to give up their seniority and the prestige and power of serving in the Senate to accept a Cabinet appointment, but several former Cabinet mem-

[3] Statistics based on a survey of the new members of the Eighty-ninth Congress (1965–1966).

[4] Samuel P. Huntington, "Congressional Responses to the Twentieth Century," in David B. Truman (ed.), *The Congress and America's Future*, Prentice-Hall, Inc., Englewood Cliffs, N.J., 1965, p. 12.

bers have been elected to the Senate, including in 1971 Sens. Stuart Symington of Missouri, Clinton P. Anderson of New Mexico, and Abraham Ribicoff of Connecticut. A number of senators have resigned in the past to accept appointment to the Supreme Court, but few senators leave the Senate voluntarily except to become candidates for President or Vice President.

Until recent years, few senators have ever been chosen by their political party to be nominees for President. The two major parties have customarily turned to the governors of the states instead of the Senate in choosing their presidential nominees. From 1900 to 1960, only one Senator, Warren G. Harding of Ohio, who was not regarded as a leading member of the Senate, was nominated to be President, but during this period seven governors were presidential nominees. During the 1960s, however, all presidential nominees of both major parties were senators or former senators; and in 1972 the leading candidates for the Democratic presidential nomination were members of the Senate. The Senate has become the training ground for presidential candidates. Their experience in national and international affairs prepares them for the responsibilities of the Presidency. Senators have often been chosen as nominees for Vice President.

Despite the necessity for running for reelection every two years, election to the House of Representatives is attractive primarily to younger persons who have previously held public office and aspire to a political career. The member who is elected from a safe district and can count on continued reelection over a long period has a good chance of advancing to the chairmanship of a standing committee or an important subcommittee, provided his party is in power when he has achieved the required seniority. The positions of great power and prestige. in the House are almost invariably filled by members who were elected at a young age from safe districts, usually from one-party areas. Election to the House is not attractive to older persons who have achieved success and recognition in their chosen profession or business, which they would have to give up for the uncertain political career in the House and the unlikelihood that they will advance to a leadership position.

Few members of the House ever achieve national recognition or become widely known outside their own districts. The more ambitious run for the Senate after serving several terms; about a third of the members of the Senate are former members of the House. Some run for governor or mayor of a large city when the opportunity presents itself, but the opportunities for advancement to higher public office are limited. No member of the House since 1900 has been nominated for President by his party, and only two members, Speaker Champ Clark in 1912 and Speaker John Nance Garner in 1932, were serious contenders for the nomination. Lame-duck members are often appointed to federal offices or to judgeships in recognition of their services to the party, but few voluntarily resign to accept an administrative appointment.

The freshman member of the House is usually assigned to one of the least desirable committees in which he has little or no interest or opportunity to be of service to his district. After he has acquired seniority he can transfer to a more desirable committee, but not necessarily his first choice. He soon discovers that the House is run by a small number of its senior members and that until he has acquired considerable seniority he will have little influence. His advancement depends upon continued reelection by his district; if he should be defeated his political career is probably at an end. If he comes from a competitive district, the swings of political parties may bring about his defeat, and if the opposing party controls the legislature he may be redistricted out of office. And the longer he has served in the House, the more difficult it is for him to return to his former profession or business and start a new career.

It has been said that membership in the House of Representatives is a stepping stone only to reelection to the House of Representatives. The House would be much more attractive to able young men and women if it provided greater opportunities for advancement to higher political positions and permitted members to render distinguished service to the country without having to wait for years to achieve seniority. After having served in the House for several years, few members are willing to give up the seniority they have acquired to accept other positions. Those who aspire to higher office almost invariably make the break after serving two or three terms. Few members whose service is interrupted ever come back.

AGE   The Constitution provides that representatives shall be at least 25 years of age and senators 30 years. The average age of all mem-

TABLE 1   Age distribution of new members of Congress, 1971

AGE	SENATE		HOUSE	
	Number	Percent	Number	Percent
30–39	1	9.1	9	16.0
40–49	6	54.5	27	48.3
50–59	3	27.3	16	28.6
60 and over	1	9.1	4	7.1
	11	100	56	100

bers of both houses in 1971 was 52.7 years, a slight decline from 1951 when it was 53 years (see Table 1).[5] The average age of senators in 1971 was 56.4 years and that of representatives was 51.9. The average age of senators entering the Senate in 1971 was 46.2 years and the median age was 44; the average entering age of new representatives was 46.8 and the median age was 47. Although the average age of senators in 1971 was 4.6 years older than average of representatives, the freshman senators were younger than freshman representatives. This may indicate a trend to elect older persons to the House than formerly. The increased salary of a member of Congress, which is now $42,500 annually, and the greater allowances for staff and expenses doubtless have made service in the House more attractive to persons of more than 50 years of age.

OCCUPATIONS   Approximately two-thirds of the members of each house of Congress are attorneys (see Table 2). It may be noted that attorneys also constitute by far the largest occupational group in state legislatures, but not in the legislative bodies of other countries. Attorneys as a rule are more highly motivated politically than members of other professions and businessmen, and moreover are better able to combine a professional career with politics. Many attorneys serve in the legislature or hold other state or local offices, which are the logical stepping stones to a career in Congress. Training in the law is

[5] The statistics are from *Congressional Quarterly Weekly Report*, vol. 29, no. 3, Jan. 15, 1971.

TABLE 2 Occupations of members of Congress, 1971

	HOUSE (percent)	SENATE (percent)
Law	54	65
Banking or business	33	27
Teaching	14	11
Agriculture	8	13
Journalism	7	7
Other	4	3

Source: Computed from *Congressional Quarterly Weekly Reports,* vol. 29, no. 3, Jan. 15, 1971. Many members are classified in two or more occupational groups.

valuable to the legislator, and the experience gained in representing others gives the attorney a better understanding of the varied interests and problems of society. However, it may be questioned whether such a large proportion of legislators should be drawn from one profession. Ideally, the legislature should be composed of persons who as a group are broadly representative of society. The primary contribution of the legislator is not as an expert but as a layman, aware of the problems and needs of society, who bring the layman's judgment to important policy decisions. When legislative committees need expert information and advice they should secure it from persons whose expertness is unquestioned rather than from their own members.

Despite the overrepresentation of rural areas in the House, only 8 percent of its members gave agriculture as an occupation, and many of these are probably "gentlemen farmers" whose main occupation is law or business. Organized labor exerts a strong influence on the actions of both houses, but there were only three labor officials in the House and none in the Senate. In addition to the above occupational groups, 82 percent of the members of the House and 99 percent of the senators listed "Public Service-Politics" as an occupation, thus indicating that the vast majority of members of each house look upon continued service in Congress or other public office as a career.

Studies comparing the backgrounds and characteristics of members of Congress with executive leaders in business and industry and in government show significant differences. Of the senators holding office between 1947 and 1957, 64 percent were raised in rural areas or small towns and only 19 percent in metropolitan areas, but 52 percent of the presidents of large corporations grew up in metropolitan centers.[6] The percentage of senators who were raised on farms was approximately three times as great as that of executive leaders in government and business. Forty-one percent of senators continued to live in their home town, but only 12 percent of corporation executives did so. Nearly three-fourths of government and business executives, but only one-fifth of congressional leaders, moved from one region of the country to another. After graduating from college or university, the typical future member of Congress returned to his home town or vicinity and pursued a political career, advancing from local office to the state legislature and then to Congress, but the typical business or government executive secured employment in a metropolitan area and worked for one or more national organizations, frequently changing his residence.

"Businessmen, lawyers, and bankers are found both in Congress and the administration. But those in Congress are likely to be small town businessmen; small town lawyers, and small town bankers."[7] Congressmen, especially members of the House, tend to be locally oriented, while business and government executives tend to be nationally oriented. "If there is one maxim which seems to prevail among many members of the national legislature", wrote Sen. Richard Neuberger, "it is that local matters come first and global problems a poor second—that is, if the member of Congress is to survive politically."[8]

RESIDENCE REQUIREMENTS   The Constitution requires that members of both houses of Congress reside in the state which they represent, but no length of prior residence is required. It is often mistakenly assumed that members of the House of Representatives must be residents of the congressional district from which they are elected, but such residence is dictated by custom and tradition rather than the

---

[6] The following account is taken from Huntington, "Congressional Responses . . .," pp. 14–15.

[7] *Ibid.*, p. 14.

[8] Quoted by Huntington, *ibid.*, p. 15.

Constitution. There have been a few instances in large cities of the election of members who were not residents of the district, but usually the candidate who is not already a resident of the district establishes residence on the eve of announcing his candidacy. In the great majority of districts, long-term, bona fide residence is demanded by the voters of candidates for Congress. A newcomer would be called a "carpetbagger," which would ordinarily assure his defeat.

Candidates for the United States Senate in the great majority of cases are long-term residents of the state; many are natives. In 1964, however, precedent was broken when Robert Kennedy, a legal resident of Massachusetts, who had resided in Washington, D.C., for a number of years, took up residence in New York, announced his candidacy for the Senate, and was elected. As Attorney General he was widely known in New York and had lived in the state as a youth. The fact that he only recently had established residence in the state did not prevent his election to the Senate in the Democratic landslide of 1964. Pierre Salinger, press secretary of Presidents Kennedy and Johnson, returned to his native state of California and won the Democratic nomination for the Senate, but was defeated in the election. Both candidates were accused of being "carpetbaggers."

The custom that members of the House must be prior residents of the districts which they represent is unlikely to be changed, except in large cities, where token residence may be accepted. The tradition that requires local residence leads to an undesirable parochialism and has other unfortunate effects. A member is tied to his district; if defeated, his political career is usually at an end. As James G. Bryce observed in his classic study, *The American Commonwealth,* there are many districts that do not raise statesmen. There are other districts where able and promising persons who aspire to a public career have no opportunity to be elected to Congress because they belong to the minority party in the district or the incumbent member of Congress is unbeatable. In Great Britain, where local residence is not required, attractive candidates are "adopted" by other districts that are seeking candidates. The local-residence tradition in the United States, which is demanded by local pride, makes it more difficult for the major parties to recruit able and promising candidates and limits the choice of voters to residents of the district.

TENURE   Since about 1900 there has been a marked increase in the length of service of members of both houses of Congress. Before 1900, usually about half of the members elected to the House of Representatives had never served in Congress before, and only a third of the senators served more than a single term. In the 10 years ending in 1966, the turnover in each new Congress averaged only 14.6 percent in the House and only 11.2 percent in the Senate. In 1971, the turnover in the Senate was 11 percent and in the House 12.9 percent. A hundred years ago, it was the practice in many congressional districts to pass the job around, electing a new congressman every two years. Abraham Lincoln, who was elected to Congress in 1846 and served a single term, wrote a friend at the end of his term that "If nobody else wishes to be elected, I could not refuse the people the right of sending me again."[9] Evidently someone else wanted the job, for Lincoln did not run for reelection. In 1900, only 9 percent of the members of the House had served 10 years or more; by 1971, it had increased to 41 percent; in 1900, only 1 percent had served 20 years or more, but by 1971 the number had increased to 13.6 percent.

Instead of being a body of amateur legislators who served for only a few years, which was true of both houses as late as 1900, Congress has become a body of career legislators who devote full time to the job and expect to continue their service until they retire or are retired by the voters. Presidents and department heads change frequently, but the chairmen and ranking minority members of committees in both houses of Congress have been in office for many years. In 1971, the chairmen of the 10 most important Senate committees had an average of 24.7 years of service in the Senate, while the chairmen of the 10 most important committees of the House had served an average of 33 years.

Through long tenure, members of Congress become experienced legislators, and through continued service on the same standing committees they become well informed on the legislative subjects dealt with by the committees. It is doubtful, however, whether extended service adds much to the competence of a member.

[9] Neil MacNeil, *Forge of Democracy: The House of Representatives,* David McKay Company, Inc., New York, 1963, p. 124.

The greatly increased tenure of members, however, is not an un-mixed blessing. Under the rule of seniority, each house is ruled by its senior and usually elderly members, who, as a rule, are elected from safe states or districts that are removed from the problems and issues that concern metropolitan areas where two-thirds of the people re-side. New members of the House, irrespective of their abilities, have little influence until they have attained seniority. As a result, the work of the House is not enhanced by the contributions that could be made by new, younger members with fresh ideas. The slow advancement of members of the House under the inflexible rule of seniority makes membership unattractive to able and ambitious persons who are un-willing to mark time for years until their elders retire.

COMPENSATION   Members of Congress receive a salary of $42,500 annually, plus generous retirement provision and substantial allow-ances for staff and other expenses. Each member is assigned a well-equipped suite of offices in one of the five congressional buildings near the Capitol. The senior members whose offices are located in the new Senate office building or the Rayburn office building for members of the House have spacious and plush office suites, but those in the older buildings do not fare so well.

Each member of the House receives a staff allowance of $133,500 to $140,500 annually, which he may spend as he wishes. Most of his staff work in his Washington office, but usually one or two are as-signed in his district to an office that handles constituent problems. Each member receives an allowance to cover the rental of one or more offices in his own district or is provided with an office in a federal building. In addition, he receives allowances for travel, long-distance telephone calls, telegraph, stationery, postage, and the like. He also may use his official frank to mail without charge official letters and publications to constituents and others.

The allowances to senators are higher than to members of the House and are graduated on the basis of the population that they represent. Senators from the more populous states receive a staff allowance that enables them to employ several professional staff members and 25 to 50 clerical employees to handle the correspon-dence, constituent services, and other calls upon the senators from the largest states. Senators from the larger states receive several thousands of letters weekly from constituents and others, many of which have to be followed up with the departments.

It may appear that the salaries and allowances of members of Congress are generous, for they are far larger than those of the legislators of other countries, but senators whose obligations are heavy find it difficult to make ends meet. Members of Congress report that they make many trips to their home district during congressional sessions that are not covered by their travel allowance. Many maintain two residences, one in their home district or state and another in Washington. They receive many invitations to make speeches or attend meetings dealing with problems in their district that require their presence, usually without any compensation. But the greatest expenses of members of Congress are for maintenance of political fences between elections and campaign expenditures for reelection. Members of the House are elected every two years, which for many members means that they must be continually campaigning for office. Campaign expenditures today may run as high as $100,000 or more for members of the House and a million dollars or more for senators from the more populous states. The candidate is usually expected to make a substantial contribution to his own campaign.

DESIRABLE QUALIFICATIONS The legislator need not be an expert in any function of government, but he needs to be able to draw upon and utilize the testimony and advice of experts in passing upon public policies and programs. The major contribution of the legislator is not as an expert but is rather as a "generalist" who has a broad understanding of society and its problems and of the competing interests and groups affected by government, and who has sound judgment based upon firsthand experience. A legislative body should include members with different backgrounds and abilities who are drawn from different professions and walks of life. Not all need to be distinguished citizens, for it needs followers as well as leaders. Not all of its members need to be philosophers or doctors of philosophy, but a few educators or philosophers will contribute significantly to its deliberations. It needs innovators as well as persons who are skeptical of change. It has little need for extremists of any stripe, but much need for moderates with flexible minds that enable them to consider objectively many points of view and to work out needed compromises.

The legislature does not need to mirror society with a proportionate number of members drawn from various races, religions, sections, occupations, and economic interests, as is sometimes advocated. It needs instead members who can speak for and represent all important segments of society. A banker is not necessarily the best representative of the banking interests, nor a farmer of agricultural interests, a union official of organized labor, and so on. Many groups are ably represented by persons from other walks of life. Each member of the House of Representatives today represents a constituency of approximately 467,000 population, including a broad spectrum of society: bankers, butchers, and bricklayers; rich and poor; white, black, and brown; Catholic, Jew, and Protestant; labor and management; and in many instances agricultural and urban areas. Senators represent even larger and more diversified constituencies.

Each member of Congress accordingly represents many different classes and groups of constituents, often with different and competing interests and desires. To do so effectively he needs certain skills, certain qualities of mind, traits, and abilities. He should be aware of and interested in the various problems and needs of his constituents and should be helpful but also discriminating in meeting these needs. He should be able in "getting things done," which requires good working relations not only with constituents but also with his fellow legislators, the interest groups, and the press; and he should be able to take a leading part in movements for the benefit of his district. He needs to have a serious commitment to the national as well as local interest and compassion for the unfortunate, which will give him deep satisfactions in his accomplishments and lighten his frustrations. Above all, he needs to have very high standards of integrity and personal conduct, for where decisions of great moment are made and the stakes are high, the temptations are also great. He needs to be a good politician, articulate, effective in arousing and retaining the loyalty and support of constituents, for in order to be a statesman the legislator must first be reelected. And he should never forget that the prime function of the legislature is not to represent but to govern.

THE ROLE OF THE CONGRESSMAN

Members of Congress usually classify their activities as "legislative" and "nonlegislative." The nonlegislative activities, which consist largely of serving their districts or states and constituents, are discussed in the following section. The major legislative activity of members is their service on one or more committees and subcommittees, where the real work of Congress is performed. Unless a member is assigned to an important committee of interest to the congressman and his district, he has little opportunity to contribute to the legislative process. Apart from voting on bills and amendments, attendance at the sessions of the House and Senate is perhaps the least important activity. Much time in each house is devoted to trivia unrelated to legislation under consideration; and, after a quorum is established, members drift away and attendance is poor. Ordinarily the debate on legislation is conducted largely by the members of the committee reporting the bill. Debate in both houses has so declined that it is not ordinarily well attended except when major legislation is being considered.

Members of Congress not only pass upon bills and amendments in committee and also when they come before the House or Senate for action, but they also introduce and lobby for their own bills or amendments, many of which relate to their own districts or states, but others are concerned with national issues. Formerly, important legislation usually bore the names of members who introduced it, but this custom has declined. Many members like to have their names attached to important legislation and seek the honor of introducing administration bills though they may have played no part in the drafting of the bill. Usually, an important bill is introduced by the chairman of the committee to which it will be referred.

Some members, especially senators, attract nationwide attention by their advocacy of or opposition to important pending bills. Senator William Proxmire of Wisconsin has led the opposition to the building of a supersonic airplane and also has been a leading critic of military expenditures. Senators George McGovern of South Dakota and Mark Hatfield of Oregon have been leading advocates of withdrawal of our troops from Indochina. Senator Edmund S. Muskie of Maine has for several years been the leading legislative advocate of protection of our environment. Senator Robert F. Wagner of New York was the legislative father of the Social Security Act, and Sen. George Norris of Nebraska was largely responsible for the establishment of the Tennessee Valley Authority.

In voting on legislation as well as other legislative activities, should the legislator be guided by the opinions and wishes of his constituents or should he act upon his own judgment and conscience? This is an issue that philosophers and political scientists have long debated. The classic statement that the legislator should follow his own judgment was made in 1774 by Edmund Burke, a member of the House of Commons, in a speech to the electors of Bristol:

> Certainly, gentlemen, it ought to be the happiness and glory of a representative to live in the strictest union, the closest correspondence, and most unreserved communication with his constituents. Their wishes ought to have great weight with him; their opinions high respect; their business unremitted attention. It is his duty to sacrifice his repose, his pleasure, his satisfactions, to theirs—and above all, ever, and in all cases, to prefer their interests to his own.
>
> But his unbiased opinion, his mature judgment, his enlightened conscience, he ought not to sacrifice to you, to any man, or to any set of men living. These he does not derive from your pleasure—no, not from the law and the Constitution. They are a trust from Providence, for the abuse of which he is deeply answerable. Your representative owes you, not his industry only, but his judgment; and he betrays, instead of serving you, if he sacrifices it to your opinion. ... You choose a member, indeed, but when you have chosen him, he is not a member of Bristol, but he is a member of Parliament.[10]

Legislators differ over the extent to which they should subordinate their own judgment to the opinions and wishes of their constituents. Some regard themselves as *trustees* elected by their constituents to exercise their own judgment; others regard themselves as *delegates* or *tribunes* to carry out the wishes of their constituents. Most legislators agree, however, that if legislation substantially affects the econom-

[10] Quoted in Theodore J. Lowi, *Legislative Politics, USA,* Little, Brown and Company, Boston, 1962, pp. 150–151.

ic interests of his district, or if a substantial number of influential constituents have strong opinions about it, the legislator should vote "for the district," even contrary to his own judgment, unless he feels very strongly about the issue. At times he must decide between pressure from his constituents and contrary pressures from the party leaders in Congress. Senior members usually advise the freshmen to "vote the district" when in doubt. Legislators from oil-producing states invariably support legislation allowing oil depletion tax allowances; those from mining areas support legislation beneficial to mining interests; those from farming areas support agricultural price support; members from districts where organized labor is strong support legislation favorable to labor.

On most legislation, there is no definite district interest or opinion and the legislator is free to follow his own judgment. An experienced congressman has stated that "a congressman can do pretty much what he decides to do and he doesn't have to bother too much about criticism."[11] What he thinks the district desires and is in its interest depends to a large extent on what his own opinions are. "A congressman's conception of his district confirms itself, to a considerable extent, and may constitute a sort of self-fulfilling prophecy," concludes Leonard A. Dexter. He tends to screen out opinions contrary to his own; most people who write to him support his positions. If he receives a large number of similar letters or telegrams urging his support or opposition to pending legislation, he recognizes that they have been stimulated by an interest group, which may not represent the opinions or interests of the majority of voters of the district. In evaluating such pressures he takes into account how influential and numerous the group is; and, unless they support his own judgment, he tends to discount such pressures.

SERVING CONSTITUENTS

Although the legislative duties of the new member of the House are usually light, the life of a representative is strenuous. He must conduct

[11] See Leonard A. Dexter, *The Sociology and Politics of Congress,* Rand McNally & Company, Chicago, 1969, chap. 8. The quotations are on pp. 153 and 159.

a primary and election campaign every two years, which means that he is running for reelection almost continually, especially during his early years in Congress before he is well established in his district. Instead of devoting most of his attention to pending legislation, the representative spends as much as 80 percent of his time serving his constituents, and his office force devotes nearly all of their time to handling constituent problems. "I thought I was going to be Daniel Webster," said one veteran representative, "and I found that most of my work consisted of personal work for constituents." [12]

Serving their constituents and looking after the interests of the district or the state is an important part of the work of members of both houses and is a "must" in order to be reelected. A common comment by experienced legislators is that the voters of their district are little concerned with how they vote on legislative measures, but they are much concerned about what the congressman does for his district and whether he takes care of the requests of his constituents in their dealings with the government departments. The member of the House receives a stream of calls, letters, and telegrams from leading citizens in his district. The job of the congressman in serving his district has greatly increased in recent years because of the growth of federal programs, which today are of vital importance to every congressional district. The member may have little prestige and influence in Washington, but he is an important person in his own district. He works with various groups to perfect local programs and projects for the benefit of his district and to secure federal appropriations for them. If local authorities are seeking a federal grant for urban renewal, public housing, flood control, rapid transit, hospital, or other projects, they seek the active cooperation of their representative and the senators from the state. When federal funds are allocated for the construction of a new post office building or other federal project in the district, it is the congressman who makes the public announcement, though he may not have had anything to do with getting the funds. If the poultry raisers in the district are going bankrupt because of low prices, he joins forces with congressmen from other districts similarly affected in

[12] Charles L. Clapp, *The Congressman: His Work as He Sees It,* The Brookings Institution, Washington, D.C., 1963, p. 51.

an effort to secure legislation or administrative action that will rescue their constituents.[13]

One of the tasks of the congressman is to secure federal offices, installations, and public works in his district, which provide added employment, enhance the economy, and also help to reelect the congressman. Incumbent congressmen often campaign for reelection citing the large federal expenditures that they have secured for the district. Senator Clinton P. Anderson, a highly respected member of the Senate, stated in a newsletter to his constituents in 1958:

> Thanks to Uncle Sam our state enjoys a greater proportion of depression-proof wage earners than any other state. One out of every five persons in New Mexico derives his income directly from the government. The national figure is one in fourteen. Twenty-seven percent of all payroll income in New Mexico comes from government payrolls. . . . All signs point toward continued expansion of government activities in New Mexico. I know that my efforts are directed constantly toward that end.[14]

Appropriations for river and harbor improvements, often without economic justification, have long been called "pork," and the omnibus appropriation for this purpose has been called the "pork barrel," for it has something for almost all congressmen. Rivers and harbors have been dredged and improved for practically nonexistent traffic. Economically sound and desirable flood-control projects provide a great boon to the affected local landowners, for the cost is largely paid by the federal government. Economy-minded members of Congress privately criticize the waste of federal funds on uneconomic public works projects, but nevertheless vote for the appropriations in order to secure funds for their own projects, a procedure known as "logrolling." Senator Paul Douglas of Illinois attempted without success several years ago to cut some of the more flagrant items of pork from the appropriations, but received no support from other senators, who

---

[13] For a graphic account of the strenuous life of the representative, see Clem Miller, *Member of the House,* Charles Scribner's Sons, New York, 1962, especially pp. 74–77.

[14] *New York Times,* Apr. 28, 1958.

invited him to cut the appropriations for his own state and let theirs alone. James G. Bryce, in his classic work on American government, written in 1888, commented on the "vast sums wasted on useless public works," concluding:

> Under the system of congressional finance here described America wastes millions annually. But her wealth is so great, her revenue so elastic, that she is not sensible of the loss. She has the glorious privilege of youth, the privilege of committing errors without suffering the consequences.[15]

The location of federal military installations, hospitals, and other field offices require the approval of Congress, which means in fact the approval of the House and Senate committees that pass on legislation authorizing the installations, and the appropriations committees of both houses. As a result, the chairmen and senior members of these committees have a powerful voice in determining locations; many of the installations are placed in their districts, or in other districts that they approve. They become not only the recipients of federal largess for their own districts, but dispensers of favors to other congressmen. States with the most senior members of these committees secure the lion's share of federal offices, laboratories, hospitals, and other installations. The state of Georgia was highly favored in the location of military installations over a period of years when its senior Senator, Richard Russell, was chairman of the Senate Armed Services Committee and at the same time chairman of the Appropriations Defense Subcommittee, and Rep. Carl Vinson, also from Georgia, was chairman of the House Armed Services Committee. Representative Richard Bolling of Missouri declared that if the state of Georgia received one more military installation "it would sink."[16]

Members of Congress are deluged with requests from constituents, which they must handle promptly in order to retain the constituent's support. Their offices are organized to service constituents; many

[15] *The American Commonwealth,* The Macmillan Company, New York, 1888, vol. 1, p. 244.
[16] Richard Bolling, *House Out of Order,* E. P. Dutton & Co., Inc., New York, 1966, p. 87.

members have a rule that constituent mail must be answered within 24 hours. If a veteran fails to receive his pension check, he requests his congressman to intercede in his behalf; if a soldier or his family desires a discharge, they ask their representative to help get it; if a constituent wants to be appointed postmaster or rural mail carrier, he writes to his representative (often several want the same job); if a civil service employee from the district thinks that he has been treated unfairly, he may take his grievance, real or imagined, to his representative; if a local business firm wants a government contract, the congressman lends a helping hand. Members of Congress welcome such requests and often solicit more constituent business, knowing that these services bring additional votes in following elections.

Many constituent requests are for information that is easily supplied; others, however, involve case work concerning veterans' benefits, social security, military discharges, and the like, which require a great deal of staff work. The offices of senators and representatives usually include persons who are specialized in handling such case work. If the constituent is unable to secure prompt action by the government agency, a letter or telephone call from the congressman's office will expedite action. Most agencies have special procedures to assure prompt action on congressional requests.

Despite the large amount of time required to handle the requests and complaints of constituents, most members of Congress believe that this is an important service and one that greatly aids them to be reelected. Citizen complaints may give the congressman an insight into the practical operation of government programs and provide a means of correcting bureaucratic action (or inaction) by government departments. Many representatives are content to devote practically all of their time to constituent business, but others feel that such work cuts into time badly needed for attention to legislative business.

Members of Congress commonly refer to services that they render their constituents as "running errands," but in many cases what the constituent wants is not information or assistance but pressure upon the government agency to accord him preferred treatment to which he is not entitled. Often the constituent misrepresents the facts. Some members scrupulously avoid putting pressure on executive departments to secure preferred treatment for constituents, but others are not so scrupulous.

It has been proposed by some members of Congress and others that the federal government should establish an office similar to the famous *ombudsman* in Scandinavian countries, which investigates citizen complaints about the action or failure to act by a government official or agency. This institution has worked admirably in rectifying arbitrary official acts or delays. The large majority of complaints are dismissed after investigation as unwarranted, but if the *ombudsman* finds that the complaint is justified, the government or the official, as a rule, makes restitution and takes steps to prevent recurrence.[17] It has been contended by proponents that a similar institution would relieve members of Congress of much of the heavy load of constituent business by providing an agency that is staffed to make an impartial, judicial investigation of their complaints, but the great majority of congressmen have no desire to be relieved of the job of intervening with the departments in behalf of constituents, which is so rewarding as a vote getter. The Joint Committee on the Organization of Congress rejected the proposal in 1966 on the questionable ground that members of Congress cannot delegate their constituent-service function to others.

THE ELECTION
OF A CONGRESSMAN

NOMINATION   In order to be elected to Congress, the candidate must win the nomination of one of the two major political parties. Independent candidates are rarely elected today. In order to secure a good committee assignment, which is so important to the member, he must be at least nominally a member of one of the major parties. Although the party label is essential to be elected to Congress and to become an effective member, party discipline in Congress is weak. After a member is elected, he is free to oppose party policies and programs, as long as he maintains the support of the voters and the party leaders in his own district. The American voter likes his congressman to be rather independent of his party and to follow his own judgment and the wishes of the district rather than those of the national party lead-

---

[17] See Donald C. Rowatt (ed.), *The Ombudsman,* Allen and Unwin, London, 1965.

ership. If he is a strong supporter of the national party leadership, he is usually accused by his political opponent of being a "yes man" or a "rubber stamp."

The nomination of the majority party is a prize eagerly sought by aspiring politicians, except in districts where the incumbent, who is usually regarded as unbeatable in the primary of his own party, is running for renomination. The nomination of the minority party in safe congressional districts, however, usually goes begging. Aspiring politicians do not seek the nomination if the chances of election are slim, for it involves raising a considerable sum of money for campaign expenses and conducting a grueling campaign. The party leaders of necessity draft a reluctant candidate, who accepts the nomination as a service to the party, hoping for future reward. If there is a prospect of winning, however, there will be no dearth of candidates.

Formerly, nominations were made by party conventions, but today the direct primary is used in all but a few states, preceded in some states by an official or unofficial party convention that endorses candidates to be voted for in the primary election. In districts where the party organization is strong, the party leaders ordinarily select the candidate whom they will support, and other hopefuls withdraw from the race, knowing that it would be futile to oppose the favored candidate and thus arouse the ill will of the party organization. In states where the party organization is not strong enough to dictate the nomination, the primary election becomes a free-for-all contest; if the chances of election are good, several candidates will usually enter the race. In most states the candidate who receives the highest vote in the primary wins the party nomination, but in the one-party Southern states a run-off primary limited to the two highest candidates is held if no candidate receives a majority in the primary.

CAMPAIGNING An incumbent senator or representative possesses many advantages over opposing candidates and in the primary of his own party is usually unbeatable. If he uses the perquisites of the office, answers his mail promptly, serves his constituents, looks after the interests of the district, and retains the support of the party leaders, he is virtually assured of reelection except when there is a pronounced shift in party strength. More than three-fourths of the congressional districts are "safe" for one party or the other, especially for an incumbent running for reelection, and hence even great shifts in party preference by voters will seldom defeat incumbents from safe districts.

The incumbent representative is widely known throughout the district, while an opposing candidate must carry on an expensive publicity campaign merely to become known by the voters of the district. The incumbent is running for reelection all the time. His most effective campaigning is conducted between election campaigns. "You can slip up on the blind side of people during an off year," stated one representative, "and get in much more effective campaigning than you can when you are in the actual campaign." [18] Representatives make frequent trips to their districts when Congress is in session, and during the recess period travel throughout the district, speaking to various groups on subjects of local interest.

Many representatives send regular letters to constituents reporting on their activities, which, between election campaigns, are usually printed by local newspapers. They also report to the folks back home by means of radio and television interviews, which local broadcasting stations may carry free as a public service except during the campaign. If a government hospital, post office, or other public work is built in the district, it is the representative who makes the announcement to the local press, though he may not have had anything to do with the decision.

Correspondence with constituents is one of the most effective means of campaigning. The representative not only has free use of the mails for official business, which includes correspondence with constituents, but also an office force paid by the government to handle such mail. He receives thousands of letters from constituents, many requesting some service or information, others expressing opinions on pending legislation. These are answered promptly and courteously in what appears to be a personal letter from the congressman. Despite the heavy load of work placed upon their office staffs, members of Congress encourage and even solicit letters from constituents, for they know that such mail pays off in the election. Many members make a practice of following the newspapers in their districts and sending out an appropriate letter to graduating high school seniors, newlyweds, and others whose names are in the news. Parents receive a letter of congratulations on the birth of a baby, with a government pamphlet on

[18] Clapp, *The Congressman: His Work as He Sees It,* p. 331.

the care and feeding of infants. The congressman who has answered his mail promptly, has served his constituents in their dealings with the government, and has secured federal projects and benefits for his district, is virtually assured of reelection.

Each candidate for representative in the primary election normally creates a personal organization to conduct his campaign. Prominent persons are asked to serve as chairmen, cochairmen, finance chairmen, and other honorary positions, but the real work is usually performed by paid or voluntary workers. Committees are set up for finance, voter registration, publicity, speakers' bureau, precinct organization, and so forth. Candidates who are running for the first time for the office ordinarily devote most of their efforts to bringing their name and candidacy to the attention of the voters, accompanied by a brief slogan that epitomizes their stands on issues or qualifications. Campaigning is carried on through newspaper publicity, advertisement, billboards, home meetings with small groups of voters, and a limited use of political rallies. Little use is ordinarily made of television and radio because of the high cost. The use of the political rally or public meeting has declined because of the difficulty in getting voters to turn out. A favorite method of campaigning today is for the candidate to meet and shake hands with a maximum number of voters, attending places where large numbers of voters congregate, such as supermarkets, factories at lunch time, street corner rallies, and the like. A mailing to the 200,000 or more voters within the district is seldom used because of the large expense.

CAMPAIGN EXPENDITURES   The cost of conducting the primary and election campaigns for Congress varies widely, depending on the size of the district, whether it is urban or rural, whether safe or competitive, whether the incumbent is running for reelection, whether the candidate is widely known in the district, whether the candidate has the support of a strong or weak party organization, and other factors. In a hotly contested primary campaign in an urban area expenditures of as much as $100,000 on behalf of each of the leading candidates are not uncommon. On the other hand, a popular incumbent is usually unopposed in his own party primary, and the nomination of the minority party in a safe district may often be had for the asking.

Except in one-party states, the candidate who has won his party's nomination faces the necessity for conducting a second and often more expensive campaign before the election. An act of Congress passed in 1925 limits campaign expenditures of candidates for the House of Representatives to $5,000, but the actual expenditures on his behalf are usually many times this amount. A representative from Westchester County, New York, reported after the 1964 election that his campaign committee raised $187,000.[19] Usually candidates report only their own personal expenses, disregarding expenditures made by others.

A campaign to reach the approximately 200,000 voters in an average-sized congressional district (including newspaper advertisements, billboards, radio and television, publicity pamphlets, paid workers, mailings, and other costs) necessarily requires a large expenditure. Many campaigns today are conducted by professional public relations firms, whose services are expensive. A single mailing to 200,000 voters would cost about $20,000. A campaign budget that allows only 25 cents per voter would cost $50,000 in an average-sized congressional district.

The campaign expenditures of candidates for the Senate, as a rule, are much higher than those of candidates for the House of Representatives. In the large urban states, an expenditure by each of the leading candidates in the primary campaign may exceed a million dollars, and an even larger expenditure is usually required in the election campaign. Even in the smaller states, campaign expenditures for the Senate of several hundred thousand dollars are not uncommon. In the 1964 primary election campaign in California, each of the two leading candidates for the Democratic nomination spent about 1 million dollars. Even larger expenditures were made by each political party on behalf of its candidate in the election campaign. In the primary campaign, the losing candidate spent approximately $250,000 for radio and television; $200,000 for mailings and literature; $100,000 for billboards; and smaller amounts for newspaper advertisement, paid employees, rent, and other items.[20] An expenditure of 1 million dollars in the primary campaign allowed only 20 cents per voter to reach the

[19] The candidate's mother and sister contributed $169,000, spreading this amount in gifts of $3,000 to each of 27 campaign committees in order to comply with the law. *The Christian Science Monitor,* Oct. 28, 1966.

[20] Alan Cranston, "A Million Dollar Loser Looks at Campaigning," *Fortune,* November, 1964.

5 million registered Democrats in the state. With campaign expenditures of this amount, the appeals to voters by both candidates consisted largely of name and face posters, a brief slogan of a few words, and six-second spot announcements on radio and television. On the basis of such appeals the voters were asked to make a choice of candidates for the Senate.

Who contributes the large sums required in primary and election campaigns of candidates for Congress? Are members of Congress placed under obligation to those who have financed their campaigns? The necessity for raising large campaign funds undoubtedly discourages many able and public-spirited citizens from becoming candidates for the House or the Senate, for they recognize that they will be under obligation to large campaign contributors. Candidates would prefer to raise campaign funds from many small contributors, but experience indicates that it is difficult, if not impossible, to raise sufficient funds by this method.

Federal and state regulations of campaign expenditures are so full of loopholes that they are practically worthless. The Federal Corrupt Practices Act does not apply to primaries but only to expenditures in the election campaign. Although a limit of $5,000 is placed on election campaign expenditures of candidates for a House seat and a limit of $25,000 on campaign expenditures of candidates for the Senate in the largest states, expenditures of many times these amounts are usually made. The limit is easily circumvented, for it applies only to expenditures by the candidate and by the committee in charge of his campaign and is not applicable to expenditures by other committees on his behalf. Limits on the amount that a contributor may give are also ineffective because large contributors split their contributions among several campaign organizations. The prohibition of campaign contributions by labor unions or corporations is also easily avoided. Only a fraction of the actual campaign expenditures is ever reported.[21]

---

[21] For further study of campaign expenditures and party finance, see Alexander Heard, *The Costs of Democracy,* The University of North Carolina Press, Chapel Hill, N.C., 1960; *Financing Presidential Campaigns: Report of the President's Commission on Campaign Costs,* Government Printing Office, Washington, D.C., 1962; Herbert E. Alexander and Laura L. Denny, *Regulation of Political Finance,* Institute of Government Studies, University of California, Berkeley, 1966.

From the above review of congressional campaign expenditures we may draw the following conclusions: (1) The amount of funds required today for campaign expenditures by candidates for either house of Congress is exceedingly high—far greater than the salary of the office for the term elected. (2) The bulk of campaign contributions comes, as a rule, from a few large contributors rather than a large number of small contributors. (3) As a result, members of Congress are placed under heavy and undesirable obligation to large contributors to their campaigns. (4) The existing regulations, including the limits on campaign expenditures, are unrealistic and ineffective. It is widely recognized that the high cost of campaigning is one of the great unsolved political problems. It has been proposed that at least a part of the campaign expenditures should be paid out of government funds, but the difficulties of administration appear insuperable. Another proposal often made is that an income tax credit with a top limit be provided as a means of encouraging small contributions.

CONGRESSIONAL REAPPORTIONMENT [22]

CONSTITUTIONAL PROVISIONS   The federal Constitution provides that the members of the House of Representatives shall be elected by the people, and that the number allocated to each state shall be apportioned on the basis of the population of the several states. The manner of electing the representatives is left to the state legislatures, subject to regulation by Congress. The number of members of the House is not fixed in the Constitution but is determined by Congress. The first Congress had only 65 members of the House, but the number was increased when new states were admitted and after each decennial census until 1911, when it was fixed at 435. Formerly Congress apportioned the members to each of the several states after each census, but an act of 1929 provides for automatic apportionment to the states following each census on the basis of population without

---

[22] The following are some recent studies of reapportionment: Gordon E. Baker, *The Reapportionment Revolution,* Random House, Inc., New York, 1966; Royce Hanson, *The Political Thicket,* Prentice-Hall, Inc., Englewood Cliffs, N.J., 1966; Malcolm E. Jewell (ed.), *The Politics of Reapportionment,* Atherton Press, New York, 1962; Glendon Schubert (ed.), *Reapportionment,* Charles Scribner's Sons, New York, 1965.

further action by Congress. After the 1970 census five states gained and nine lost seats; California gained five seats; Florida, three; and three other states each received one additional seat.

HISTORY In 1842, Congress enacted a law requiring the states that were allotted more than one representative to elect them from single-member districts. Before that time several states elected their representatives from the state at large. In 1872, Congress further regulated the election of representatives by providing that the districts should be equal in population "as nearly as practicable," and in 1901 provided that the districts should be compact and contiguous. These standards, however, were never enforced either by Congress or by the courts and were largely disregarded by the state legislatures.

In the early history of the country, when there were few cities and the vast majority of the population lived on farms and in small towns, there was little or no issue of rural versus urban representation in the legislature. Representation according to population was generally accepted in theory but not always followed in practice. The original constitutions of 36 states provided for representation in both houses of the state legislature substantially on the basis of population.[23] With the rapid growth of urban population in the latter half of the nineteenth century, however, the state legislatures, which were controlled by rural members, often refused to reapportion seats in the state legislature on the basis of population as required by the state constitution, for this would have required rural areas to give up seats to the rapidly growing cities. Those who are in power seldom willingly give up that power. In some states, as in Illinois and Tennessee, the state legislature failed to reapportion the state over a period of 50 years or more, despite great shifts and growth of population. A number of states revised their state constitutions to provide for the apportionment of one house on the basis of local governments or areas instead of population, which was the practice of several of the original thirteen states. By one device or another, the legislatures of practically all states reapportioned the state so as to maintain rural control of one or both houses of the legislature, despite the rapidly growing urban population. By the 1960s, the value of votes cast for the state legislature

[23] Advisory Commission on Intergovernmental Relations, *Apportionment of State Legislatures,* Washington, D.C., 1962, p. 10.

in urban and metropolitan areas was only half that of votes cast in rural counties.[24]

CONGRESSIONAL REDISTRICTING In redistricting the states for the election of members of the House of Representatives, it is not surprising that rural-controlled state legislatures favored rural areas. In 1962, the population of congressional districts throughout the country (except in states which had only a single district) ranged from 951,527 to 177,527. All of the 20 largest districts, which ranged in population from 951,527 to 621,379, were urban, suburban, or mixed; all of the 20 smallest districts, which ranged in population from 252,208 to 177,527, were rural. In several states, the most populous congressional district had four times as many residents as the least populous district, and in most states rural areas were substantially overrepresented on the basis of population, and urban and suburban areas underrepresented.

SUPREME COURT DECISIONS For many years the underrepresentation of urban population in the state legislatures and in Congress was widely criticized, but efforts to force the state legislatures to redistrict on the basis of population were unavailing. The courts refused to intervene, holding that reapportionment is a political decision assigned to the legislative body and hence not subject to judicial review. In 1951, President Harry S. Truman recommended legislation to Congress requiring congressional districts to be substantially equal in population. To carry out his recommendation, Rep. Emanuel Celler of New York introduced a bill that provided that congressional districts may not vary by more than 15 percent from the average of all congressional districts within a state, but the bill received little support in Congress. The failure of Congress to enact legislation to correct the serious overrepresentation of rural areas and underrepresentation of urban and suburban areas eventually led the Supreme Court to reverse a long line of decisions and to require substantial equality of population of congressional districts. It is significant that the Supreme Court rather than Congress itself acted to bring about what has been described as one of the most important reforms of Congress.

[24] See Paul T. David and Ralph Eisenberg, *Devaluation of Urban and Suburban Votes,* Bureau of Public Administration, University of Virginia, Charlottesville, 1961.

In 1962, the United States Supreme Court, by a divided vote, reversed its earlier decision and held in the famous case of *Baker v. Carr* (369 U.S. 186) that the action of the state legislature in redistricting the state, or its failure to act as required by the state constitution, was subject to review by the courts. The case arose in the state of Tennessee, whose legislature had not redistricted the state for 50 years, although required by the state constitution to do so after each census. The Supreme Court did not enunciate standards to guide the state legislatures in redistricting, but it was widely assumed that reapportionment on the basis of population would be required in at least one house of the state legislature. Lawsuits were quickly initiated in a number of states to force the reapportionment of the state legislatures. In a series of decisions in 1964, the Supreme Court held that the equal protection clause of the federal Constitution requires both houses of state legislatures to be apportioned so as to achieve substantial equality of population. In *Wesberry v. Sanders* (376 U.S. 1, 7) the Court interpreted the provision in the federal Constitution that members of the House of Representatives shall be "chosen by the people of the several States" to mean that "as nearly as practicable, one man's vote is worth as much as another's." Thus the Court enunciated the doctrine of "one man, one vote," which requires single-member congressional districts to have substantially equal population. The Supreme Court has not specified how much deviation from the average population is permissible; but, in two decisions in 1969, it set aside a redistricting act in New York that had a maximum deviation of 6.6 percent and a Missouri act in which the maximum deviation was only 3.1 percent. Unless greater deviation is permitted in the future, congressional district boundaries will necessarily divide many local communities and create highly artificial congressional districts with little or no community identity. There is grave danger that the principle of "one man, one vote" has been carried too far. Substantially equal population is important, but communities are also important and should not be divided into two or more congressional districts if division is avoidable.

Thirty-one states reapportioned their congressional districts between 1964 and 1970 to meet the standard of substantial equality of population, but the shifts in population as indicated by the 1970 census were so great that probably 46 states will have to redistrict again before 1972 to achieve substantial equality of population. Four states have only a single member of the House of Representatives. New York State, for example, which reapportioned in January, 1970, allowing a difference of only 803 persons between the most populous and the least populous district, based on the 1960 census, will have to redistrict on the basis of the 1970 census, which indicates that the most populous district has a population of 737,762, while that of the least populous district is 331,482.[25] In most states the redistricting will necessarily change the boundaries of nearly all districts.

THE GERRYMANDER The reapportionment revolution that followed the recent Supreme Court decisions has resulted in the creation of congressional districts of substantially equal population, ending the widespread discrimination against urban and suburban population, but has not ended nor will it end the political gerrymander.[26] The redistricting of the states for the election of members of Congress has long and notoriously been conducted in a highly partisan manner by the party that controls the legislature. A skillful gerrymander, as partisan redistricting has come to be called, may be of great aid to the party that redistricts the state. This is illustrated in the congressional elections of California in 1962, following the Democratic redistricting of the state in 1961. Although Democratic candidates for Congress polled only 51.8 percent of the vote cast, they won 66 percent of the seats in Congress; the Republican candidates, who polled 48.2 percent of the vote, won only 34 percent of the seats. The number of Republican votes throughout the state per seat won was 207,000, while the number of Democratic votes per seat won was only 115,000.

The effect of partisan redistricting was even more striking in Los Angeles County. The Democrats carried it by a razor-thin majority of only 7,226 out of more than 2 million votes cast, but elected 11 members of Congress, while the Republicans, with almost the same number of votes, elected only 4. In Southern and border states, the Republican party, which ordinarily polls from 30 to 45 percent of the

[25] Statistics from *Congressional Quarterly Weekly Report,* vol. 29, Mar. 26, 1971.

[26] The word "gerrymander" was coined in Massachusetts in 1812 to describe a district with a grotesque shape. A cartoonist, who noticed that the shape of one district resembled a prehistoric monster, added claws, wings, and a forked tail and called it a salamander. Because Governor Gerry had signed the bill permitting such a monstrosity, it was called a "gerrymander."

vote, is usually able to elect only one or two members of Congress from each state and in some states is unable to elect any members. In Texas, the Republicans polled 44 percent of the vote in 1962, but elected only 2 of the state's 22 members of Congress.

Several techniques are used in gerrymandering a state to gain the greatest party advantage. The party that redistricts usually attempts to concentrate a maximum number of voters of the opposite party in a few large districts, which the opposition will carry by huge majorities, and to create as many districts as possible that its candidates will carry by comfortable, but not overwhelming, majorities. By shifting areas from one district to another, with close attention to past voting statistics, doubtful districts may be turned into safe districts, and safe districts may be made doubtful. Districts may be redrawn so that incumbents of the opposite party are compelled to run from new districts that are stacked against them.

In order to create the maximum number of safe districts for the party in power, district boundaries often arbitrarily divide local communities between two or more congressional districts and combine parts of a number of separate communities into a single district. As a result, districts with grotesque shapes are created, formed out of parts of widely separated communities with little or no interests in common. There are long, narrow, "shoestring" congressional districts; others containing two large, separated areas connected by a narrow strip are known as "dumbbell" districts; and some, because of their peculiar shape, are called "saddlebag" districts. One district in California, extending from San Bernadino County in the southern part of the state to the Oregon border, is more than seven hundred miles in length.

"SAFE" DISTRICTS One of the effects of partisan redistricting is that a large majority of congressional districts are "safe" for one party. It is generally accepted that a district is safe if the winning candidate receives 55 percent of the vote. By this standard more than three-fourths of the congressional districts are safe, and less than 100 districts are truly competitive. Only a landslide victory of one party will change the results in safe districts. Incumbents from safe districts are virtually assured of reelection and long, continuous tenure, except when great shifts take place in party strength.

As long as redistricting is performed by the state legislatures, the party in control will continue to carve out legislative districts for partisan advantage. The only way in which the partisan gerrymander can be avoided is to take the function of redistricting away from the legislature and turn it over to a nonpartisan agency, or a bipartisan agency with one neutral member to avoid deadlock. Three states—New Jersey, Pennsylvania, and Hawaii—have adopted bipartisan commissions. Since a constitutional amendment would be required in all states to adopt this plan, partisan redistricting by state legislatures is apt to continue in most states.

In Great Britain, the job of redistricting is assigned to a nonpartisan boundary commission under standards prescribed by law. Districts may not vary more than 25 percent from the norm. In revising the parliamentary districts, the boundary commission not only takes into account population to achieve substantial equality, but also endeavors to form parliamentary districts that retain intact local political subdivisions and established communities wherever possible. It scrupulously avoids partisanship, which has long been characteristic of redistricting in this country.

REVIEW QUESTIONS

1. Discuss the effects of the American tradition that members of Congress must be prior residents of the district.

2. "The incumbent congressman who uses the perquisites of his office, takes care of his constituents, and answers his mail is virtually assured of reelection." Discuss.

3. "The high cost of political campaigning is one of the most serious problems of American democracy." Discuss as it applies to members of Congress.

4. Review the historical developments of legislative apportionment before the *Baker v. Carr* decision.

5. Discuss the principal effects of congressional reapportionment since 1964.

6. What are the principal methods used in the political gerrymander?

7. Criticize the effects of the gerrymander and discuss possible reforms.

3 PARTY LEADERSHIP IN CONGRESS

PARTY ORGANIZATION [1]

At the opening of each new Congress, the elected members of the two major political parties in each house of Congress meet in party caucus to choose the party officers and to decide upon committee

[1] See David B. Truman, *The Congressional Party,* John Wiley & Sons, Inc., New York, 1959; Donald R. Matthews, *U.S. Senators and Their World,* The University of North Carolina Press, Chapel Hill, N.C., 1960; Julius A. Turner, *Party and Constituency; Pressures on Congress,* The Johns Hopkins Press, Baltimore, 1951, chaps. 1–3; Hugh A. Bone, "An Introduction to the Senate Policy Committees," in Lawrence K. Pettit and Edward Keynes (eds.), *The Legislative Process in the U.S. Senate,* Rand McNally & Company, Chicago, 1969, chap. 8; Charles O. Jones, *Party and Party Making: the House Republican Policy Committee,* Rutgers University Press, New Brunswick, N.J., 1964; Randall B. Ripley, *Party Leaders in the House of Representatives,* Brookings Institution, Washington, D.C., 1966.

assignments, which are of the greatest importance to individual members. As is often said, the real work of Congress is performed by the standing committees; each member seeks appointment to the most important and powerful committees, particularly to those whose work vitally affects his district or state. The committee assignments are prepared by a committee on committees and are approved by the party caucus. Each house invariably accepts the committee assignments, including the committee chairmen, proposed by the two parties.

The party organization of the two major political parties in the Senate and the House are similar, though not identical, and consists of (1) the party caucus, or conference as the Republicans prefer to call it, of all members of the party; (2) the party leader of each house; (3) the whips, consisting of a chief whip and a number of assistant whips; and (4) several party committees, including a policy committee, committee on committees, steering committee, patronage committee, and party campaign committees. The functions performed by these party committees are not always accurately described by their titles; they vary somewhat between the two parties, and are different in the two houses. The majority leader in the House is customarily elected Speaker, the presiding officer of the House, and the majority floor leader acts as his assistant.

THE IMPOTENT CAUCUS   Formerly, each party used the caucus for discussion and determination of the party position on pending legislation; and, if a position was approved by the required majority, members of the party were bound to vote as determined by the caucus, except those who announced that they were opposed to the decision on constitutional grounds or that it was contrary to pledges that they had made to the voters. During President Woodrow Wilson's first term, the Democratic caucus played a highly important role in controlling legislation brought in by the standing committees and in passing the President's extensive legislative program. Since that time, however, the party caucus has greatly declined in strength and in use.

For many years, the caucus has rarely been used by either party to bind members. After the Speaker was shorn of his powers in 1910, there was no effective means to enforce caucus decisions of the majority party. The spread of the direct primary after 1910 greatly weakened the political party control in most states, which was reflected in the decline of party discipline in the House. For many years, the Democratic party has seldom called caucus meetings to discuss party policies and pending legislation. The Republican party, which is more united, makes occasional use of the conference to discuss issues and seek a consensus, but not to bind members. One Democratic congressman explained the reason that his party did not make more use of the caucus, saying that "all this talk about the caucus is just a dream anyway. The Democrats are so deeply split in philosophy that they cannot encourage anything that might divide them even more."[2] The split in the Democratic party between the Northern and Western liberals and Southern conservatives on civil rights, labor legislation, public housing, welfare, and expansion of the federal government is so wide that the party leaders are reluctant to call caucus meetings for fear of disrupting the fragile coalition.[3] The party leadership has preferred to keep tight control over party policies, consulting privately with party members instead of holding caucus meetings, which would give those opposed an opportunity to air their opposition. Standing-committee chairmen and senior committee members are also opposed to calling of party caucuses, which might reduce their control over legislation within their jurisdiction.

The party leaders and the committee on committees, which are different in the House and the Senate, are discussed below.

PARTY WHIPS The party whips[4] and their assistants aid the party leaders in keeping in touch with members of the party, informing them of the legislative schedule and the party position, reporting their views

[2] Charles L. Clapp, *The Congressman: His Work as He Sees It,* The Brookings Institution, Washington, D.C., 1963, p. 299.

[3] It was reported that a Democratic caucus in the House of Representatives in 1933 shortly after President Franklin D. Roosevelt had made heavy reductions in veterans' benefits resulted in such strenuous objections to these cuts that the leadership hastily adjourned the meeting to avoid open opposition to the President.

[4] The word "whip" has been borrowed from the British Parliament and is an abbreviation of the word "whipper-in" used in fox hunting for persons who "whip-in" straying dogs. The term is ludicrous when applied to the undisciplined political parties in Congress. See Daniel Berman, *In Congress Assembled,* The Macmillan Company, New York, 1964, p. 234.

to the leader, polling members before key votes, and rounding up party members when votes are taken.

Each party in the House assigns whips to the larger states and to geographical areas. The whip's job has been described by the late Clem Miller, representative of a northern California district, as follows:

> The key to effective whip action is timing. The whip is on the floor surveying the scene and weighing alternatives. He watches the Republicans to observe whether they are present in force or are hiding in the cloakroom awaiting a prearranged signal to descend on the floor. He gauges the end of the general debate and estimates the time when a vote is likely. If he puts out a call too soon, too urgently, many members will assemble, take a quick look, and then begin to fade away until there is a critical deficiency when the vote is taken. Yet he cannot defer too long, because a vote might come unexpectedly.[5]

PARTY POLICY COMMITTEES The Joint Committee on the Organization of Congress in 1945, seeking to strengthen the roles of political parties in Congress, recommended the creation of party policy committees in each house, which were intended to be an organization of party leaders to formulate broad legislative policies, but the committees have never performed this function. Because of the opposition of the House leaders, the provision was stricken in the Legislative Reorganization Act of 1946, but in 1947 the Senate adopted party policy committees for the Senate in an appropriation rider. Initially only $15,000 was appropriated for this purpose, but this amount was increased in later years and had reached a quarter of a million dollars by 1963.[6]

The Republican party in the House subsequently created a policy committee, but the Democratic party has failed to do so. The Senate Democratic policy committee is consulted by the party leader concerning the scheduling of legislation to be called up in the Senate. The staffs of the committees publish special studies and reports useful to members of the party, especially in political campaigns.

[5] *Member of the House,* Charles Scribner's Sons, New York, 1962, p. 53.
[6] Berman, *In Congress Assembled,* p. 217.

PARTY CAMPAIGN COMMITTEES Congressional campaign committees have been used by each party in the House for more than 100 years and by the parties in the Senate since the popular election of senators was instituted by the Seventeenth Amendment, which was adopted in 1913. Although each of the political parties has national headquarters in Washington, members of both houses prefer to have their own campaign committee to serve them. Congressional party leaders remain somewhat aloof from the national party headquarters, which, of the party in office, is the agent of the President. The principal function of the congressional and senatorial campaign committees is to collect funds for the campaigns and to distribute them to candidates in districts where the party has a good chance to win and financial aid is needed. The amount available to each candidate is necessarily small in relation to the high cost of campaigning today. Incumbents who have supported the party leadership are presumably favored in the distribution of funds. The committee staffs prepare studies, analyses of voting records, speeches, and other material useful to party candidates, and between elections assist party incumbents in securing publicity and in other ways.

The Senate campaign committees are drawn from senators who are not coming up for election and hence are available to assist party candidates in other states. Since all members of the House come up for reelection every two years, the members of the House campaign committee are ordinarily unable to lend a helping hand to candidates of other districts.

WHY POLITICAL PARTIES IN CONGRESS ARE WEAK

Although the political parties in Congress are notoriously weak and members are free to vote as they please on legislation without incurring party discipline, it is the parties that organize each house, elect their leaders, select the powerful committee chairmen, and make the all-important committee assignments. If the parties used this power discriminatingly it would provide a powerful sanction in strengthening the parties, but the rule of seniority, which has become more rigid since 1910, nullifies any effective use of the power by the parties.

A candidate who is elected to Congress as an independent or a nominee of a third party, which today is usually rare, can receive committee assignments only if he is accepted by one of the major parties and admitted to its caucus. In 1970, James L. Buckley, the nominee of the Conservative party, was elected to the Senate from New York with the support of the Republican national administration and many Republican leaders in New York. He was accepted by the Senate Republican caucus and given committee assignments. Senator Harry Flood Byrd, Jr., of Virginia decided against entering the Democratic primary, where he might have been defeated, and instead ran for reelection as an independent and won. When he returned to the Senate he retained his membership in the Democratic caucus, his seniority, and his committee assignments.

The majority-party leader of the Senate and the Speaker of the House, who is also the majority-party leader, are by all odds the most influential members of their respective houses, yet their formal powers are relatively small. Senator Mike Mansfield, the Democratic majority leader of the Senate, often states that he has only the powers that all senators have. Although technically correct, this statement overlooks the potent means at the disposal of a skillful majority leader to influence the votes of members of his party; these means are discussed in a subsequent section.

Members of Congress do not owe their nomination and election to the national party organization or to the congressional party leaders, but rather to party organizations in their districts or states and to their own personal following and support. The congressional party leader can do little to help them get reelected, always a prime consideration, or to defeat them. Even the President is unable to "purge" members of his party who have opposed his legislative program, as President Franklin Roosevelt learned in 1938. His announced opposition to several members who had opposed his program, although claiming to constituents that they supported it, instead of defeating them, in most instances helped them to be reelected. The congressional party leaders must win the support of party members by persuasion rather than by command, by aiding them to secure passage of their own bills, and in a variety of other ways.

The committee system of Congress in combination with the seniority rule greatly limits the power of the party leaders. Each standing committee is the master of its legislative domain; it fights strenuously to protect its jurisdiction from invasion by other committees and resists any attempt by others to direct or control its activities. The chairman and the ranking minority member are, in effect, the leaders of their respective parties with regard to legislation passed on by the committee. Instead of being advised by the party leader, they instruct him concerning party policies within their jurisdiction. Each has served from 10 to 20 years on the committee and understandably believes that he is much better informed about legislation considered by the committee than the party leader, who probably has never served on the committee. Yet they need his assistance in passing (or defeating) legislation and consult him about party strategy and tactics and are amenable to his suggestions as long as they are suggestions and not orders.

The seniority rule, which applies not only to the selection of committee chairmen and ranking minority members but also to all committee members, makes them largely independent of control by the party leadership. Once appointed to a committee, a member is entitled under the seniority rule to retain his committee assignment as long as he is reelected, whether or not he has supported the party policies, unless he voluntarily gives up his committee assignment to receive a better one. Parliaments with strong political parties do not use standing committees, each assigned to definite areas of legislation, such as are used in Congress. Strong legislative committees, each with a large degree of autonomy and with members who through long service become experts in the area of legislation assigned to the committee, are not compatible with strong political parties.

PARTY LOYALTY OF CONGRESSMEN

Despite the factors limiting the role of political parties in Congress, there are other factors that strengthen the parties. Although there are few measures on which all members of a party unite, except in organizing each house, party identification is nevertheless the single most important factor in explaining the votes of members.[7] The members of each party sit together in each house, use the party lounge rooms where they meet informally, dine together as a rule, and mix socially with other members of the party. They sit together in committees, where the real work of Congress is done, and frequently caucus in order to act in concert on pending legislation. Every member of Congress is a partisan; his advancement to positions of power and influence is as a member of a party.

Members of each party have strong reasons for working within their party and aiding it to succeed and make a record that meets with public approval. Those who advance to positions of great power and prestige as chairmen of committees or subcommittees do so only if their party is in power. They play the leading roles in developing, revising, and enacting legislative policies of great importance to the nation. The ego satisfactions of members of the minority party, who are biding their time until their party comes into power, are not comparable.

Under each party umbrella are some members whose views on issues differ widely from those of the national party leadership. In all states the party label or nomination, ordinarily the label of the majority party in the state or district, is necessary in order to be elected, but once elected the member of Congress is not required to support the party platform or to vote with the congressional party leadership. If he is a member of the party in office, he is free to vote for or against the legislative measures of the President. In fact, he needs to vote against some of the President's legislation in order to avoid attack in the following election as a "yes man" of the President. The congressional party leaders have no effective means to discipline members who fail to vote in accord with the dominant interest and opinion of their constituents.

There are a few members in each house who consistently vote with the opposite party, but rarely is any attempt made by the party leadership to discipline such members. The late Sen. Harry Byrd of Virginia,

[7] See Frederick A. Cleaveland and Associates, *Congress and Urban Problems*, Brookings Institution, Washington, D.C., 1969, p. 371; also David R. Mayhew, *Party Loyalty Among Congressmen*, Harvard University Press, Cambridge, Mass., 1966, and the works of Randall B. Ripley and Charles O. Jones, which are cited in footnote 1.

for example, voted more consistently with the Republicans than any Republican member and, in addition, did not support any Democratic candidate for President after 1948; yet he retained the powerful chairmanship of the Senate Finance Committee and no effort was made to discipline him. In 1965, the House Democratic caucus took the unusual step of stripping Rep. Albert W. Watson of South Carolina, who had supported Goldwater for President in 1964, of his seniority. He thereupon resigned from Congress and was reelected as a Republican by an overwhelming majority. Rep. John Bell Williams of Mississippi was also deprived of his seniority for the same reason, and the Democratic caucus refused to restore it in 1967. In previous elections, however, other Southern Democrats and Adam Clayton Powell of New York City openly supported the Republican presidential nominee without being disciplined.

The fact that a few members of each party vote more often with the opposite party than their own—and most members of each party occasionally vote against the party—does not mean that parties have little or no influence on lesislative votes. The great majority of members of both parties seek to go along with the party leadership whenever possible and vote against it reluctantly when the party position is contrary to their own deeply held convictions or to public opinion in their own states or districts. Studies of the voting behavior in each house indicate that when the parties divide, 70 to 90 percent of the members usually vote with their party. The fact that members of the party are free to vote against the party position often delays action until events bring about a consensus or force the adoption of a compromise.

THE INFLUENCE
OF CONSTITUENTS

One of the most important factors influencing the votes of members of Congress, competing with party loyalty at times, is the interests of their districts or states. When party loyalty and district interest coincide the results are highly predictable. The new member of Congress soon learns that to get a dam, hospital, or other federal installation for his district, which will increase employment and promote prosperity, or to secure legislation to help the poultry raisers or peanut farmers of his district, he must combine forces with members from other districts who are wholly unconcerned about the plight of the poultry industry in California or the peanut farmers of Georgia, but are very much concerned about the decline of employment in the textile industry in their own districts, or the cutback in employment in the aerospace industry, or the decline in the price of cotton, corn, wheat, tobacco, silver, copper, or whatever their districts produce. The happy solution is legislation that benefits at least 218 districts, thus assuring a majority vote. To secure benefits for his district, the member finds that he must vote for the benefits for other districts, even though he may regard some of them as unwise and wasteful. Urban and suburban congressmen often vote for legislation favorable to the farmer, even if it increases the cost of living of their constituents, in order to secure the votes of members from agricultural districts for legislation beneficial to urban and suburban districts.

The Democratic and Republican parties significantly differ in their philosophy concerning federal expenditures for the benefit of "interested" districts. This difference in philosophies is summarized by David R. Mayhew in his perceptive study of congressional party loyalty:

> It can be said that the Democratic party in these years was transcendently a party of "inclusive" compromise. ... Some congressmen wanted dams, others wanted mineral subsidies, others wanted area redevelopment funds, others wanted housing projects, still others wanted farm subsidies. As a result, the House Democratic leadership could serve as an instrument for mobilizing support among all Democrats for the programs of Democrats with particular interests. ... Republicans who characterized the Democratic party as a "gravy train" were quite right. John McCormack, not ordinarily known as a philosopher, expressed with great insight ... a philosophy of what the Democratic party was and what bound it together. McCormack persistently argued that, on domestic economic questions, each segment of the party relied upon and deserved the support of all other segments of the party, and that a summation of the programs of the various party elements constituted the national interest.[8]

In contrast, concludes Mayhew, the Republican party is a party of "exclusive" compromise, devoted to the interests of business, free

---

[8] *Party Loyalty Among Congressmen,* p. 150. Reprinted with permission of Harvard University Press.

enterprise, and economy in government, and opposed to the expansion of the federal government.

Wherever possible, most Republican congressmen opposed federal spending programs and championed policies favored by business. Thus, whereas "interested" minorities in the Democratic party supported each other's programs, each "interested" minority in the Republican party stood alone. The Republican leadership responded to the legislative demands of each minority by mobilizing the rest of the party to oppose them.[9]

As would be expected, defectors in the Republican party, who often voted with the Democratic majority, were members from districts with predominant "interests," for example, farming districts interested in the price of agricultural products, urban and suburban districts interested in urban renewal, housing, mass transportation, environment, welfare, and labor legislation.

In his study of party leaders in the House, Randall B. Ripley stated his findings: "Among the Republicans, rural members were the most loyal. Urban members were the next most loyal, and suburban members were the least loyal." Republicans from rural districts were the most conservative of the party and had the fewest "interested" districts, and hence were the most loyal of the party. Among the Democratic members, however, the ranking in order of party loyalty was in reverse order. Representatives from suburban districts were the most loyal, from urban districts next, and rural members ranked lowest in party loyalty.[10]

OTHER FACTORS INFLUENCING VOTING BEHAVIOR

In addition to party loyalty and constituents' interests, there are various other factors that influence the votes of members. On most legislation, there is no party position or district interest; the member is free to follow his own judgment and may be influenced by other cues in arriving at his decision. Organized interest groups, which are numerous and highly influential, play an important and even essential role in

[9] *Ibid.,* p. 155.
[10] *Party Leaders in the House of Representatives,* pp. 155–156.

the legislative process, yet most members deny being influenced by pressure groups. The function of pressure groups, which is discussed in Chapter 5, is primarily to organize the group and to represent it before legislative and administrative bodies.

Legislators are greatly influenced by other legislators. When not fully informed on the merits of legislation under consideration (which is often the case), most legislators follow the lead of the party's senior members of the committee that reported the bill. Often the issues are highly complex and only members of the committee are able to form an intelligent judgment.

In Congress and out, members of Congress belong to various groups and associations, which influence their choices. The party members of the larger state delegations usually meet regularly to be briefed on pending legislation, and they tend to vote alike. There are various groups of like-minded members who meet regularly, often at breakfast or lunch, to discuss legislative issues and to exchange ideas and information. Illustrative of such groups is the Democratic Study Group discussed below.

THE DEFEAT OF THE SST APPROPRIATION IN 1971: A CASE STUDY

The defeat of the appropriation to continue the building of two super-sonic transport airplanes (SST) in March, 1971, is an example of cross-party voting and the effects of local interests and public opinion on congressional votes. In December, 1970, the Senate defeated an appropriation for the SST in a fight led by the maverick senator from Wisconsin, William Proxmire, who for 10 years had unsuccessfully opposed appropriations for the SST. The House had previously approved the appropriation, which had the support of the leadership of both political parties and was backed by the administration. After the defeat in the Senate, the bill was sent to a conference committee of the two houses, which reported a reduced appropriation at the end of the year. After a deadlock and filibuster in the recessed session in January, 1971, the opponents agreed to an appropriation to permit work on the SST to be continued until March 30, 1971.

The airplane and engine manufacturers (Boeing of Seattle, General Electric, and subcontractors in various states), assisted by the aviation industry and 31 unions of the AFL-CIO, with the active support of the administration, mounted a massive lobbying campaign to save the SST. It was reported in the press that $350,000 was raised for the campaign. News commentators forecast that the campaign would succeed and Congress would appropriate the necessary funds. For 10 years the House had held firm in voting appropriations for the SST despite mounting criticisms. Senator Proxmire expressed doubts that the opponents could defeat the SST appropriation in the face of the well-financed campaign to save it.

Advocates of the appropriation contended that if the construction of the SST were discontinued this country would lose its leadership in the aviation industry. Great Britain and France had jointly built the Concorde, a supersonic transport, and Russia also had a supersonic transport completed. In the House debate, Republican leader Gerald Ford declared that abandonment of the project would cost the country not only the 834 million dollars already spent by the government, but also would result in the loss of 13,000 jobs immediately and 150,000 jobs that would be created when the plane went into production and the loss of billions of dollars in foreign exchange in the future. Seattle and Los Angeles were already having serious unemployment because of the decline of the aerospace industry.

Opponents of the SST had previously centered their attack on the ground that the cost of the project was out of all proportion to the benefits received; they condemned it because of the huge sum required to build a plane that would transport only a relatively few very wealthy persons, while the urgent needs of the cities were being neglected. In hearings conducted by a subcommittee headed by Senator Proxmire, leading scientists testified that fleets of SSTs would reduce the ozone in the upper atmosphere and might increase the incidence of cancer. Testimony concerning the danger to the environment was widely publicized in the press; and, although such testimony was discounted by other scientists who saw no real danger, members of Congress received a flood of mail opposing the appropriation to continue construction of the SST. Several inquiries on the feasibility of the SST that had been conducted by expert commissions were reported to be unfavorable, but they were never released by the White House.

The SST appropriation was supported in the House by the leadership of both political parties. Democrat Sidney Yates of Illinois led the opposition. When the vote on the amendment was called, Yates demanded tellers with clerks, the new procedure adopted by the House at the opening of the session under which names are recorded. Previously names were recorded only on roll-call votes when the House was in regular session; no record was made of how each member voted on important amendments when the House was sitting as a committee of the whole. In the vote on the SST appropriation amendment, members would have to answer to their constituents back home on how they voted. Nearly 100 percent were present and voted, an extraordinarily high vote on an amendment. The appropriation was defeated by a vote of 215 to 204; 115 (47 percent) of the Democrats voted for the appropriation and 131 (53 percent) against; 89 (51.5 percent) of the Republicans voted for and 84 (48.5 percent) against. The nearly equal vote for and against by the Democrats was expected, but the vote of 48.5 percent of the Republicans against in opposition to the administration and the Republican leadership of the House was surprising. The newly elected members of Congress, voting 31 to 18 against, provided the majority that defeated the appropriation. Congressmen of both political parties from southern California, where much aerospace industry is concentrated, voted overwhelmingly for the appropriation, but a majority of Democrats from northern California voted against it.

A week later, the Senate defeated the appropriation by a vote of 51 to 46. Democrats voted 34 to 19 against, and Republicans voted 27 to 17 in favor. The SST prime contractor, Boeing, is located in Seattle, and the two Democratic senators from Washington voted for and led the fight for the appropriation. However, the two California Democratic senators voted against, despite the large majority of representatives of both parties from southern California who voted for the appropriation. Among the Republicans who voted against the appropriation were the Republican whip and several senior and highly respected senators. The President made a last-minute appeal to senators believed to be undecided, but three of the four who called on him at the White House on the day of the vote cast their votes against the appropriation.

THE SENATE

POWERS The United States Senate is by all odds the most powerful legislative body in the world. Although in its early history the Senate was somewhat overshadowed by the larger and popularly elected House of Representatives and, for several decades, limited itself largely to acting upon bills already approved by the House, it clearly has become the more powerful and prestigious body. Its debates and the hearings of its committees are frequently reported in the press, which is seldom true of the House. A leading author has admiringly referred to it as the "Citadel" and the "Institution."[11]

The Senate and the House of Representatives have equal legislative powers, but the Senate has certain exclusive powers over foreign affairs and executive appointments to higher offices that give it preeminence in the control of the executive branch. All treaties with foreign powers must be approved by a two-thirds vote of the Senate. Because of this power, Presidents and Secretaries of State have learned from experience that it is advisable to consult with the Senate leaders, especially members of the powerful Senate Foreign Relations Committee, in advance of important foreign policy decisions. It has become the practice of the President to appoint senators as members of delegations to international bodies and as representatives of the United States in conferences with other countries. The Foreign Relations Committee of the Senate plays an influential role in determining foreign policies, but the corresponding committee of the House of Representatives has much less influence.

The Senate possesses another power that enhances its influence in foreign affairs, namely, its power to advise and consent to the President's nominations for Secretary of State and other top officials of the State Department, including ambassadors to foreign countries and officers of the Foreign Service. In choosing a Secretary of State, the first consideration of the President is whether the person of his choice can get along with the leaders of the Senate. It is for this reason that in the past this post has been offered to senators who are held in high esteem by their colleagues.

---

[11] William S. White, *Citadel: The Story of the U.S. Senate,* Harper & Row, Publishers, Incorporated, New York, 1956.

The power of the Senate to pass upon the President's nominations adds greatly to its authority, as well as to the political patronage wielded by individual senators of the President's party. Under the unwritten rule of "senatorial courtesy," the Senate will reject a nominee who is objected to by a senator from the state where he is to serve. The effect of the rule is to transfer the power of nomination of federal field officers from the President to the senators of each state, provided they are members of the President's party. This gives the senators important patronage and is a symbol of power in their states. The requirement of confirmation gives the Senate a powerful sanction over the appointments of the President and a control over executive officers that is not enjoyed by the House of Representatives.[12]

The framers of the Constitution evidently intended that the House of Representatives, the more numerous body whose members were directly elected by the people (it was not until 1913 that members of the Senate became popularly elected), should have primary responsibility for voting taxes, and hence provided that revenue bills must originate in the House. This provision has been extended by custom to appropriations as well as revenue bills. The House will not consider any bill that raises revenue or votes appropriations unless it originated in the House. The fact that the Senate cannot originate finance bills, however, does not lessen its power in passing on such measures when they are taken up by the Senate. It is free to revise finance bills as it sees fit, to increase or reduce appropriations, to strike items and add new ones, and has equal powers with the House when finance bills passed by the two houses in different form are sent to conference.

THE ESTABLISHMENT The Senate is run by a ruling group of influential senior members who customarily work together, make the key decisions on many, but not all, legislative policies, and collectively maintain and defend the customs and traditions of the Senate. The leaders of this group, which is called the "establishment" by former Sen. Joseph S. Clark of Pennsylvania and the "Inner Club" by William S. White, hold positions of great power and prestige, including the

[12] See Joseph P. Harris, *The Advice and Consent of the Senate*, University of California Press, Berkeley, California, 1953.

majority and minority party leaders, the whips, the chairmen and ranking minority members of the most important standing committees; and they constitute a majority of each party committee on committees. It should be noted, however, that the establishment is not identical with the party leadership group. There are committee chairmen who are not a part of the establishment, though they cooperate with it, and there are some members of the establishment who have not yet achieved the seniority that would entitle them to the key positions of power.

Senator Clark criticizes the establishment on the grounds that it is conservative, unrepresentative of the membership, undemocratic, and unresponsive to the problems and needs of an urban society.

> The Senate establishment . . . is almost the antithesis of democracy. It is not selected by any democratic process. It appears quite unresponsive to the caucuses of the two parties, be they Republican or Democratic. It is what might be called a self-perpetuating oligarchy.[13]

His major criticism is that the establishment, through its control over committee assignments, has placed a majority of conservatives on the most important committees and thereby has been able to prevent liberal legislation from being passed by the Senate.

In his book praising the Senate and its customs and traditions, William S. White writes that at times a mere frown or question by members of the inner club is sufficient to defeat a motion on the floor, as though a "wind had blown upon it from the inner club."[14] White's inner club and Clark's establishment are essentially the same, although one writes about the group with admiration and the other with criticism, and each emphasizes different characteristics. The ruling group, whether it is called the establishment or inner club, includes members from both political parties, who on the majority of issues are able to work together in harmony and accommodation. It includes liberals as well as conservatives, but the latter predominate; it in-

[13] *The Senate Establishment,* Hill and Wang, New York, 1963, p. 22; see also his *Congress: The Sapless Branch,* Harper & Row, Publishers, Incorporated, 1965, chap. 6.

[14] *Citadel,* p. 87.

cludes senators from all parts of the country, but senators from the South form the central core and are the main keepers of the customs and traditions of the Senate. Many members of the establishment are elected by one-party states, which by tradition reelect their senators until they achieve great seniority that elevates them to positions of power and influence. Seniority alone, however, is not enough to qualify a senator for membership in the establishment; some senior senators are not a part of the ruling group, while others with little seniority are accepted.

The dominance of the Senate by Southern senators when the Democratic party is in control is indicated by the fact that the chairmen of 8 of the 10 most powerful and influential standing committees of the Ninety-second Congress (1971–1972) were from the South. The chairmen of all the six top standing committees in member preference—Foreign Relations, Appropriations, Finance, Armed Services, Agriculture and Forestry, and Judiciary—were Southerners.

FOLKWAYS OF THE SENATE

One perceptive student describes the institutional patriotism expected of members of the Senate thus:

> Senators are expected to believe that they belong to the greatest legislative and deliberative body in the world. They are expected to be a bit suspicious of the President and the bureaucrats and just a little disdainful of the House. They are expected to revere the Senate's personnel, organization, and folkways and to champion them to the outside world.[15]

The new member serves an apprenticeship when he enters the Senate. He receives one good committee assignment but his other assignment is to one of the least important committees. In the committee room he sits at the end of the table. During his first year, he is expected to be seen but not heard. Senators who violate this rule incur the displeasure of their colleagues and may never be accepted into the inner circle. They are expected to show respect to their elders

[15]Matthews, *U.S. Senators and Their World,* p. 101.

and to perform the boring tasks that other senators want to avoid. If they would gain the respect of their colleagues, they need to specialize in certain areas of legislation, to acquire the reputation of being a work horse—not a show horse—and to conform to the customs and traditions of the Senate.

A cardinal rule of the Senate is that members shall always show proper courtesy to other senators. If a senator is called away from Washington at the time an important bill on which he wishes to speak is to be taken up, it will be put over at his request. Senators customarily refer to each other as "the distinguished Senator from ———" or "the able and learned Senator from ———." Senators seldom pass up an opportunity to speak in the highest terms of their colleagues, even those for whom they hold no high regard. Another custom is to follow the rule of reciprocity by voting for legislation sought by colleagues to benefit their states, in return receiving their votes for projects in one's own state.

Under the custom of reciprocity, the Senate has voted funds for many public works projects of dubious merit—including many not included in the President's budget—especially for river and harbor improvements. Even senators who advocate economy seek federal funds for projects of questionable merit in their own states, feeling that they must play the game in order to be reelected. The rule of reciprocity is not limited to public works projects but also applies to other legislation such as the tariff, farm price supports, various subsidies, private bills, and other programs of benefit to particular states.

After a senator has served his apprenticeship, he is free to speak on the floor of the Senate and to participate fully in the work of the committees and subcommittees to which he is assigned; but if he would become influential and be accepted by the establishment, he must observe the customs and folkways of the Senate. The influential senator, aware that few votes are changed by debate, seldom speaks on the floor of the Senate, and when he speaks it is on a subject about which he is well informed and his words carry weight with his colleagues. The loquacious senator who speaks frequently and on many subjects usually talks to empty seats and the gallery. The Senate frowns upon the publicity seeker, though it is tolerant of members who must secure publicity that they need for reelection.

PARTY LEADERS IN THE SENATE

The Senate is organized by the two major political parties, which make the committee assignments, so important to individual members, and select the majority and minority party leaders.[16] The Vice President, who is the official presiding officer, is not a member of the Senate and, in contrast to the elected Speaker of the House, he has little influence on its actions. He is not selected by the Senate and has no part in the distribution of positions of power and influence, particularly committee assignments; and his rulings on parliamentary questions may be overridden by a majority vote. The President pro tempore of the Senate, the elected alternative presiding officer, is largely an honorific office. In the frequent absences of the Vice President, freshmen senators, whose duties are light during their first two years in office, are called upon to preside.

The majority and minority party leaders are elected by the party caucus of their respective parties. The rule of seniority is not followed by the parties in the selection of their leaders. Junior members are often elected. Lyndon B. Johnson was chosen leader of the Democratic party in 1953 after serving only four years. After the death of the late Sen. Everett Dirksen in 1969, his son-in-law, Sen. Howard H. Baker, Jr., of Tennessee, was a candidate for Republican leader, although he had served only two years in the Senate and was supported by the conservative wing of the party. He was defeated by Sen. Hugh Scott of Pennsylvania, who was serving his second term. Senior senators who hold important committee chairmanships, most of whom are more than 70 years of age, do not want to give up their prestigious positions to undertake the arduous duties of majority leader.

The single most powerful officer of the Senate is the majority-party leader, who is recognized ahead of other senators when he seeks the floor and has a leading voice in determining the agenda of the Senate.

[16] The leading works on party leadership in the Senate include David Truman, *The Congressional Party,* John Wiley & Sons, Inc., New York, 1959; Matthews, *U.S. Senators and Their World,* chap. 6; Julius Turner, *Party and Constituency: Pressures on Congress,* The Johns Hopkins Press, Baltimore, 1951; and Ralph K. Huitt, "Democratic Party Leadership in the Senate," *American Political Science Review,* vol. 55, pp. 333–334, June, 1961.

By custom, he makes the motions concerning the bills or other business to be taken up, ordinarily after consultation with other members. He guides the debate, especially on administration bills, and frequently takes a leading part, assisting committee chairmen and other senators in securing the passage of their bills. When the President is of the same party, the majority leader maintains close contacts with his office and seeks approval of the President's legislative program. He is the center of a communications network that enables him to keep in close touch with the progress of legislation in committees, to know which bills individual senators wish to have enacted as well as their attitudes on pending legislation.

The leadership of the Democratic party in the Senate is highly centralized in the hands of the elected leader, who holds the four top leadership positions: floor leader, chairman of the party conference, chairman of the party policy committee, and chairman of the party steering committee. The party conference or caucus is a meeting of all senators of the party, which is held at the opening of each new Congress to organize and to approve the assignments of party members to the standing committees of the Senate. The party policy committee is consulted by the leader about which bills will be taken up by the Senate; the party steering committee decides upon committee assignments of party members, subject to approval by the party conference. In the Republican party, leadership is corporate; the party leader does not serve as chairman of the conference or the party committees, these positions being held by other senators.

The functions of the majority leader are numerous and his influence is great, but his leadership is based on custom rather than the rules of the Senate. He works closely with the minority leader, whom he usually consults before making motions to take up bills or other business, or to close debate and vote on the pending legislation. Majority leaders often disclaim having any power other than that possessed by all senators, and assert that their only means of directing the work of the Senate is persuasion rather than power.

The only real power available to the leader (said Senator Lyndon B. Johnson, the most effective party leader in the history of the Senate) is the power of persuasion. There is no patronage; no power of discipline; no authority to fire senators like a President can fire his members of Cabinet.[17]

Although the majority leader lacks formal powers, he has other means at his command to influence the actions of senators of his party and even those of the opposite party. His most important power is his voice in making committee assignments, despite the limits imposed by the custom of seniority. Senator Lyndon B. Johnson's decision in 1953 to give each freshman member at least one important committee assignment, and his ability to persuade some senior members to give up one of their choice committee assignments, was one of his most important decisions. It placed in his debt each entering class of freshmen senators of his party every two years. As senators acquire seniority, they seek transfers to more desirable committee assignments, in which the leader may help them. At times he may persuade a senior senator to give up one committee assignment and accept another in order to pave the way for another senator to secure a coveted assignment. He also can be very helpful in securing the passage of bills pushed by senators for the benefit of their states or appropriations for projects that will help them to be reelected.

When, as is usually the case, the same party is in control of the Presidency and the Senate, the majority leader works closely with the President to secure passage of his legislative program, and his influence is enhanced by that of the President and the administration. He may be instrumental in securing favors for his colleagues that would not otherwise be available. His role as majority leader is necessarily somewhat ambivalent. He is expected to steer the President's legislative program through the Senate, securing the passage of as much of it as possible, compromising its provisions when necessary to secure adoption. He advises the President and his aides on what can be passed and what cannot, and it is understood that he speaks for the President. But if he would be influential, he must be more *senatorial* than *presidential* in his allegiance. His influence would be seriously weakened if he were regarded as the President's man. The majority-party leader must occasionally differ with the President to show his

[17] "Leadership: An Interview with Senate Leader Lyndon Johnson," *U.S. News & World Report,* June 27, 1960.

independence, which is necessary to maintain the leadership of his party in the Senate and may be necessary to be reelected in his own state, for voters like their senators to be somewhat independent. When President Franklin D. Roosevelt in a veto message denounced a tax bill passed by Congress, Alben W. Barkley resigned as the Senate majority leader and strongly attacked the President for his harsh statement on the bill. President Roosevelt, understanding the politics of Barkley's attack, urged the Democrats to reelect him majority leader, which they did by unanimous vote. Barkley's declaration of independence assured his reelection by the voters of Kentucky. Senator Mike Mansfield, Democratic leader since 1961, has frequently expressed views on the Vietnam war and withdrawal of American troops from Europe that differ from those of the administration.

Lyndon B. Johnson, Democratic leader from 1953 until he became Vice President in 1961, who was extraordinarily successful in holding the party together and securing the passage of legislation which he favored, is the best example of an effective party leader and the techniques he uses to influence the votes of his colleagues.[18] Johnson was a master in legislative maneuvering and in finding compromises that would receive the necessary majority vote. He made little use of the party conference or caucus, or the other party committees that he controlled, preferring to maintain direct, personal contacts with the members of his party. It is said that he talked to every Democratic senator every day. Unquestionably, he kept in close touch with them and was fully aware not only of where each stood on important legislation but what legislation each wanted. He often aided senators of both parties in getting their bills approved and collected on these favors when he needed their votes, but he did not ask senators to vote contrary to their deeply held convictions or for a vote that would injure them politically in their own states. He was a master at the art of persuasion and invariably knew the appeal that would be most effective for each senator. "Let us reason together" was his approach with colleagues. Often he used other senators to win the support of colleagues with whom he had little influence and was often able to win over the key senator whose lead would be followed by others.

[18] See Huitt, "Democratic Party Leadership in the Senate."

Johnson's task as Democratic leader was made easier by the fact that he had no responsibility for securing the enactment of President Dwight D. Eisenhower's legislative program, though he worked amicably with the President in international affairs and defense. His network of communications enabled him to know what action the Senate would take, and when he made a motion his colleagues were aware that "Johnson's got the votes." This created an aura of infallibility, which enhanced his influence.

Like other effective party leaders, Johnson took a middle-of-the-road position on social and economic issues, and, though often criticized by liberal Democrats for his neutrality, he was able to work harmoniously with all factions of the party. He was conservative enough to work with the Southern conservatives and sufficiently liberal to work with the Northern liberals. He used the combined staffs of the Democratic policy committee and the Democratic conference, plus his own staff as a senator, to supplement his network of communications and to work on legislation.

The role of the minority leader is less demanding and influential than that of the majority leader. Minority-party senators, as a rule, are more desirous of collective party action than are senators of the majority party. The Republican party in the Senate, currently in the minority, makes greater use of the party committees and the party caucus than the Democrats. The Republicans use the policy committee to discuss pending legislation and issue statements of party policy to members, but the Democrats use it only as an advisory body, which the party leader may consult in determining which bills will be taken up.

The party leaders must work within the framework of largely autonomous standing committees and the tradition of seniority, which seriously restrict their power. They do not select nor can they remove the powerful chairmen of standing committees, who are selected automatically under the inflexible rule of seniority, irrespective of whether they are in agreement with or opposed to the national party policies that are acted on by the committee. It is not uncommon for a committee chairman to be opposed to the policies of his own party and to use his considerable powers to block legislation recommended by the President and supported by the congressional party leadership.

PARTY LEADERS IN THE HOUSE OF REPRESENTATIVES

THE SPEAKER   The Speaker, who is the presiding officer of the House of Representatives, is elected by the members at the beginning of each Congress.[19] Each party selects its candidate in a party caucus before the opening session of the House, when the candidate of the majority party is elected in a straight-party vote. The candidate of the minority party becomes the leader of that party. This is one of the very few straight-party votes in the House during the session. When there is a change in party control, the former minority leader is chosen by his party to become Speaker, and the former Speaker steps down and becomes the minority party leader. Thus Reps. Sam Rayburn of Texas, Democrat, and Joseph W. Martin, Jr., of Massachusetts, Republican, switched positions several times between 1947 and 1955, as the two parties alternately controlled the House.

The Speaker is the recognized leader of his party in the House and has a far more influential role than the Vice President as presiding officer. He is expected as majority party leader to facilitate the passage of the legislative program of the party. In contrast with the Speaker of the British House of Commons, who exercises his powers as presiding officer in a nonpartisan manner (although he is a party member), the Speaker is not expected to be nonpartisan in his rulings; but he is expected to be fair and to observe the precedents of the House in passing upon parliamentary questions. His role is to see to it that the business of the House is conducted in an orderly manner and to prevent obstruction by the minority party.

Formerly, the Speaker of the House of Representatives was the single most powerful member of either house of Congress, second in prestige and power only to the President. His powers arose because

---

[19] Leading works on the party leadership in the House include Richard Bolling, *House Out of Order,* E. P. Dutton & Co., Inc., New York, 1966; Mary P. Follett, *The Speaker of the House of Representatives,* Longmans, Green & Co., Inc., New York, 1896; Paul D. Hasbrouk, *Party Government in the House of Representatives,* The Macmillan Company, New York, 1927; Randall B. Ripley, *Party Leaders in the House of Representatives,* Brookings Institution, Washington, D.C., 1967; David B. Truman, *The Congressional Party,* John Wiley & Sons, Inc., New York, 1959.

of the inability of the House to conduct its work without strong leadership. Until 1911, the Speaker enjoyed three great powers that made him master of the House: (1) He appointed the standing committees and named their chairmen. (2) He appointed the Rules Committee, which ran the House, and served as its chairman. (3) He could recognize or decline to recognize members who desired the floor. Because of these powers the Speaker was often referred to as a "czar." As long as the Speaker could name the members of the standing committees, he could dictate the course of legislation. Several times he delayed appointing the committees (once for 245 days) until his legislative program had been passed. The last of the Speakers under the old order, "Uncle Joe" Cannon of Illinois, dominated the House for years and dictated what bills it would pass. In 1910, a group of "insurgents," led by George Norris of Nebraska, succeeded in having the Speaker stripped of the first two powers. No longer was he permitted to name the members of the standing committees—the selection of which is of such great importance to individual members—or to serve as the chairman of the Rules Committee. He retained the power to rule on parliamentary questions, to assign bills to committees (which in practice is usually done by the parliamentarian), to recognize members who desire the floor (usually by prearrangement), and to appoint select and conference committees.

The revolt of 1910 greatly reduced the official powers of the Speaker and increased those of the standing committees and the committee chairmen, who no longer were subject to control by the Speaker. The Rules Committee became the most powerful body in the House, for it could block consideration of bills reported by the standing committees, but its power was essentially negative. The House was thus deprived of any leader who had sufficient powers to lead a large body of 435 representatives.

Despite the reduction of his powers, the Speaker continued to be the recognized leader of his party in the House. A highly respected and able Speaker, such as the late Sam Rayburn of Texas, who served 16 years as Speaker before his death in 1961, was able to provide leadership and to direct the course of legislation through exercise of influence rather than power. Despite his great prestige and the many favors that he had rendered to members of Congress, Rayburn was unable to prevent the Rules Committee from blocking consideration of liberal measures that a majority of members of the House favored. In 1965, the House revised its rules to provide that the Speaker could bypass the Rules Committee and bring legislation recommended by a standing committee before the House for its consideration, but two years later this revision of the rules was repealed.

MAJORITY LEADER The House majority-party leader is not in fact the leader of his party, but is rather the chief lieutenant of the Speaker. He ordinarily advances to the Speakership when that office is vacant. Thus Sam Rayburn, John W. McCormack, and Carl Albert were Democratic majority leaders before being elected as Speaker, and Joseph W. Martin was Republican leader before being elected Speaker in 1947 and 1953. The role of the House majority leader is similar to that of his Senate counterpart, except that his powers are much less. He is consulted by the committee on committees concerning committee assignments, he works closely with the party whips, aids committee chairmen when their bills are being considered by the House, and often speaks for the party on pending legislation. Neither he nor the Speaker has as much control over the agenda of the House as the Senate majority leader exercises.

The minority-party leader of the House performs the same functions as his counterpart in the Senate. He speaks for the party, leads the attack on the legislation of the majority party, and is expected to take the initiative in presenting alternatives to the majority party's legislative measures.

DEMOCRATIC STUDY GROUP

Within each party there are informal groups of like-minded members who meet frequently to discuss pending legislation and to plan strategies and cooperative efforts. The most notable of these is the Democratic Study Group, which was formed by Northern liberal Democrats in September, 1959, after the liberal wing of the party had suffered a number of defeats at the hands of the coalition of conservative Southern Democrats and conservative Northern Republicans.[20] The two

[20] See Bolling, *House Out of Order,* pp. 54–58, and Miller, *Member of the House,* pp. 130–131.

wings of the conservative coalition were well organized and disciplined; they acted in concert and did not fail to have their members on the floor when important votes were held. Although a large number of Democratic liberals were elected from Northern and Western states in 1958, the group was unorganized, poorly disciplined, and often its members were not on the floor when key votes were taken. The conservative coalition held a majority of seats on the most powerful committees, including the Rules Committee, and, having a large proportion of the senior members, had defeated liberal measures.

The name "Democratic Study Group" was chosen to allay the fears of the Democratic party leadership that it was an attempt to set up a rival organization. The group meets for discussion and study and has a staff, prepares research reports, fact sheets, and position papers that members find useful. It is, however, more than a study group; its most important function is to see to it that its members are on the floor and vote when important legislation is taken up. For this purpose it has its own whip organization, which supplements that of the party.

The DSG has been the spearhead in the drive for liberal legislation since its formation and led the fight to curb the powers of the conservative coalition on the Rules Committee, which for years had successfully blocked liberal legislation. It cooperated with the Democratic leadership in passing the legislative programs of Presidents Kennedy and Johnson, despite the opposition of conservative Southern Democrats. It has also pressed for better committee assignments for liberal Democrats.

Only time will tell whether the DSG will continue as an effective, unofficial party organization. Similar groups in the past have usually disappeared within a few years, and some commentators express the view that the DSG will also be short-lived. The Democratic leadership initially viewed the DSG with some apprehension, fearing that it may harden the division within the party, but welcomed its assistance in rounding up the votes needed to pass the President's program.

REVIEW QUESTIONS

1. Describe the party organization of the House and Senate and the functions of each office or committee.

2. Compare the influence of party loyalty and constituents on voting by members of Congress.

3. Why are political parties weak in Congress?

4. Discuss the Senate "establishment" and criticisms of it.

5. Describe the "folkways" of the Senate.

6. What are the powers and means used by the Senate majority leader to secure approval of the party's legislative program?

7. What are the powers and influence of the Speaker? What powers were taken from him in 1910?

8. Why is not greater use made of the party caucus in the two houses of Congress?

9. What are the functions of the congressional campaign committee?

10. Describe the Democratic Study Group and how it works.

4 THE COMMITTEE SYSTEM

"Congress in session is Congress on exhibition, whilst Congress in its committee rooms is Congress at work" is even more true today than it was in 1883 when it was written by Woodrow Wilson in his classic study of Congress.[1] The real work of Congress is done today by its 38 standing committees and increasingly by their more than 250 subcommittees. Each legislative committee is assigned a broad class of legislation, such as agriculture, armed services, foreign affairs, taxation, and the like. It is in these committees and their numerous subcommittees that legislative policies are deliberated and decisions are reached, subject to the approval of the two houses.

[1] *Congressional Government,* 15th ed., Houghton Mifflin Company, Boston, 1900, p. 79.

FUNCTIONS OF COMMITTEES

The work load of Congress today is so great that standing committees and subcommittees are needed to consider the 14,000 bills introduced annually and to perform the other functions assigned to committees (see Table 3). Many of the bills are lengthy and complex, usually controversial, and of national significance; others are largely technical

TABLE 3   Standing committees of the Senate and House*

SENATE	HOUSE
Foreign Relations	*Exclusive Committees*
Appropriations	Appropriations
Finance	Rules
Agriculture and Forestry	Ways and Means
Armed Services	*Semiexclusive Committees*
Judiciary	Agriculture
Commerce	Armed Services
Banking, Housing and Urban Affairs	Banking and Currency
Rules and Administration	Education and Labor
Interior and Insular Affairs	Foreign Affairs
Post Office and Civil Service	Interstate and Foreign Commerce
Public Works	Judiciary
Government Operations	Post Office and Civil Service
District of Columbia	Public Works
Labor and Public Welfare	Science and Astronautics
Aeronautical and Space Science	*Nonexclusive Committees*
Veterans' Affairs	District of Columbia
	Government Operations
	House Administration
	Interior and Insular Affairs
	Merchant Marine and Fisheries
	Internal Security
	Standards of Conduct
	Veterans' Affairs

*The Senate Committees, except the last two, are listed in order of member preference. See Donald R. Matthews, *U.S. Senators and Their World,* The University of North Carolina Press, Chapel Hill, N.C., 1960, p. 153. The House Committees are listed alphabetically within each of the three groups.

and uncontroversial amendments to clarify or correct previous legislation; and still others are private bills affecting only the named individuals. The first task of the committee is to decide which of the numerous bills referred to it shall be considered. The decision rests ordinarily with the chairman, who must be persuaded that the bill is important, is needed, and has sufficient support to assure its passage. If the chairman decides that the bill should be considered he refers it to one of the subcommittees to conduct hearings. If the decision of the subcommittee after conducting hearings is favorable, it proceeds to consider the bill in detail, section by section, and revises it in accordance with the wishes of the members of the subcommittee. It then reports the bill to the full committee, recommending that it be approved and reported to the parent house.

In addition to considering proposed bills, standing committees and their subcommittees conduct hearings and investigations on problems within their jurisdiction—one of the most important functions of Congress—and inquire into the administration of departments and agencies within their jurisdiction, which is called "oversight." Investigations are considered in Chapter 6.

Each house of Congress also uses select, special, and joint committees for a variety of purposes, but, as a rule, only standing committees are authorized to report legislative bills to the parent house. Each house usually accepts and approves bills reported by its standing committees with little if any change. This is due partly to the large volume of legislation and the wide range of subjects covered and to the tradition that has developed over the years to delegate great authority and power to the standing committees. The committees and subcommittees have become the most important power centers of Congress.

Many bills that are considered by Congress today are so detailed and technical that only the members of the standing committee that reported them are in a position to have an informed judgment concerning their provisions, a fact that members of the House often point out when bills are debated on the floor. Although there may have been substantial differences among the members of the committee over the provisions of a bill under consideration, after they have compromised their differences the members of the committee ordinarily join together in opposing amendments offered by others when the bill is taken up by the House or Senate.

If the parent house seldom revises the bills reported by its committees, the standing committees of the other house do not hesitate to do so and usually invite the sponsors of bills to submit suggested revisions. As a result, the bills passed by the two houses often differ substantially, and a conference committee is required to compromise these differences and present an identical bill to each house. The conference committee, as we shall see in a later section, plays a vital role in the legislative process.

No other major legislative body in the world makes such extensive use of standing legislative committees as Congress or grants them such great autonomy and independence. Under the rule of seniority (discussed below), which is an important feature of the committee system in Congress, members of standing committees continue to serve on these committees as long as they remain in Congress, unless they seek assignment to another committee. Through long service they become experts on the subjects of legislation that come before the committee, and through seniority they acquire power and prestige. Because of their great powers and relative independence of control by the parent house, the standing committees of Congress are often referred to as "little legislatures." Today this could be said also of many of the subcommittees.

Only a few of the approximately 14,000 bills introduced annually in Congress are ever considered by the committee to which they are referred. In Woodrow Wilson's words, when a bill is referred to a committee, it "crosses a parliamentary bridge of sighs to dim dungeons of silence from whence it will never return." Unless a bill is favored by the chairman of the committee and is considered to be of urgent importance, even though a majority of committee members are favorable, it will seldom be considered. Even bills recommended by the President as a part of his legislative program may not be taken up by the committee to which they are referred if the chairman is opposed. Bills on taxation and social security recommended by the late President Kennedy, for example, were not taken up for several years because of the opposition of Rep. Wilbur D. Mills of Arkansas, chairman of the House Ways and Means Committee.

The negative power of a congressional committee to reject bills referred to it is far greater than its power to bring about their enactment. As a rule, bills that are not reported die in committee. Each house has rules by which it may withdraw a bill from a committee that has failed to report it, but members of the committee concerned vigorously oppose such withdrawal as an encroachment on the functions of the committee. Members of other committees, jealous of the prerogatives of their own committees, are understandably reluctant to support a discharge motion, even though they may favor the bill that is being bottled up in committee. The standing rules of the House make it extremely difficult to discharge a committee from further consideration of a bill. A discharge petition must be signed by a majority of all members (218), and when the petition is taken up, a majority of those present and voting must vote to take the bill from the committee and make it the order of business of the House. It is difficult to get 218 members to sign a discharge petition because even members who favor proposed legislation regard such a petition as an invasion of the prerogatives of the standing committee. Although many discharge petitions have been filed in the House to force a committee to report bills, only two bills have been enacted into law through this procedure in the past 25 years. The threat of a discharge petition, however, has been sufficient in some instances to force the committee to report a bill that a majority of members favored.

A committee of the Senate may be discharged from further consideration of a bill at any time by a majority vote of the members present and voting, but the Senate also is very reluctant to take this action. Several times the Senate has found it necessary to bypass the Judiciary Committee, which under the chairmanship of Sen. James O. Eastland of Mississippi has become known as the "graveyard of civil rights legislation." For example, in 1960, a civil rights bill was attached as an amendment to an inconsequential bill permitting the leasing of land at Fort Crowder, Missouri, which was before the Senate.

COMMITTEE ASSIGNMENTS

The rules of the Senate limit members to service on only 2 committees of a list of 13 of the more important standing committees—except senior members who in 1970 were already serving on 3 committees on the list—and 1 of the following 4 less desirable committees: District of Columbia, Post Office and Civil Service, Rules and Administration, and Veterans' Affairs. Senators who were serving on 2 or more committees in the second group in 1970 were permitted to retain their committee assignments. Senators may also serve on one select or special committee and one joint committee. Approximately half of the senators serve on 2 standing committees, and half on 3. Assignments to the most highly preferred committees, especially Foreign Relations, Appropriations, and Finance, are usually given only to senior members, while freshmen and junior members are assigned to less desirable committees.

The House rules classify committees into three classes: exclusive, semiexclusive, and nonexclusive. Members assigned to exclusive committees—Appropriations, Rules, and Ways and Means—may not hold another committee assignment; those assigned to a semiexclusive committee may also be assigned to one nonexclusive committee. A majority of House members hold only a single committee assignment, but a fairly large number hold two. In addition, many members also serve on joint committees, and most members serve on several subcommittees.

In the Senate, as Table 3 indicates, the most sought-after committees are Foreign Relations, Appropriations, and Finance, while in the House the committees on Appropriations, Ways and Means, and Rules are most preferred. Assignment to one of these House committees carries great prestige and power and requires hard work and devotion to duty. Few members are appointed to one of these House committees until after they have served several terms.

Some members of the House seek assignment to a "bread-and-butter" committee that will enable them to promote the economic interest of their own districts and thereby facilitate their reelection. Representatives from farming districts seek appointment either to the committee on Agriculture or to the Appropriations Committee, where they hope to be appointed to the subcommittee that passes on agricultural appropriations. Members from the West often seek appointment to the Interior and Insular Affairs Committee; those from districts with shipyards seek assignment to the committee on Merchant Marine and Fisheries; while those from areas that have military installations, or hope to secure such installations, head for the committee on Armed Services or Appropriations. As far as possible, the committee on committees of each party endeavors to give members the committee assignments that will be most helpful to them in being reelected. The effect is to stack many of the committees with members who have axes to grind for the benefit of their districts.

A study of the House Agriculture Committee in 1958 showed that 33 of the 34 members represented agricultural districts.

As might be expected, congressmen from constituencies with significant interests in farm policy make up the membership of the House Agriculture Committee. In 1958 there was but one exception to this rule—Victor Anfuso, Democrat from Brooklyn. Thirteen of the 19 Democrats came from areas where tobacco, cotton, peanuts, and rice are the principal commodities. Republican Committee members came from areas producing corn, hogs, small grain, wheat, and areas where farming is diversified.[2]

The committee worked principally through its 18 subcommittees, 10 of which were assigned specific commodities, such as cotton, tobacco, wheat, peanuts, dairy products, and the like. With very few exceptions, members were assigned to the subcommittees for the agricultural products of their own districts; for example, members from cotton-producing districts were assigned to the cotton subcommittee, those from wheat-producing districts to the wheat subcommittee, and so on.

The fact that many standing committees and appropriations subcommittees of Congress consist largely of members who pass upon programs that benefit their districts or states, and hence are not representative of the membership of the parent house or of the country, is a serious defect of the committee system. It explains in part why the general interest of the country is often subordinated to the special interests of particular areas or economic groups.

In the Senate, the Republican party uses a committee on committees of 10 members, which makes the assignments, subject to approval by the party caucus. The Democratic steering committee, headed by the party leader, makes the committee assignments of party members. In the House, the Republican party uses a committee on committees consisting of one member from each state that has a Republican representative (each member having one vote for each Republican representative from his state). The senior Republican representa-

[2] Charles O. Jones, "Representation in Congress: The Case of the House Agriculture Committee," *American Political Science Review,* vol. 55, pp. 358–367, 1961.

tive from each state is customarily elected as a member of this committee. The Democratic members of the Ways and Means Committee serve as the committee on committees for the Democratic party. The committee on committees not only assigns new members to committees, but also passes upon requests of old members for transfers to more desirable committees. The list of committee assignments, including committee chairmen, is routinely approved by the party caucus and subsequently by the House or Senate.

There are never enough choice committee assignments to go around, and in the scramble for favored assignments, new members usually have to take what is left over after senior members have been assigned. Consequently, the freshman member often is assigned to a minor committee in which he has little or no interest and which affords him little opportunity to serve his district. Senator Lyndon B. Johnson, when he was floor leader of the Senate, instituted the practice of giving each new senator one "good" committee assignment, a practice that has since been followed to some extent by both parties. The competition for committee assignments is much more keen in the larger House of Representatives, and freshmen members are seldom assigned to one of the more important committees.

The rule of seniority is generally, but not always, followed in making transfers of members to preferred committees. To secure an assignment to one of the major committees, the House member must gain the confidence and respect of his seniors and be accepted as a "responsible" member; that is, one who is considerate of the rights and opinions of others, moderate in his position on legislative issues, and willing to compromise; who conforms to the traditions and customs of the House and wins in his own district by a comfortable majority.[3] The late Speaker Sam Rayburn's advice to newcomers was that "to get along, you must go along."

The use of the Democratic members of the Ways and Means Committee as a committee on committees has been criticized because they are not truly representative of the party membership and tend to favor conservatives in making the committee assignments. Most members of the Ways and Means Committee are from safe, one-party

[3] See Nicholas A. Masters, "Committee Assignments in the House of Representatives," *American Political Science Review,* vol. 55, pp. 345–367, June, 1961.

districts, and have served in the House an average of nearly 10 years before being appointed to the committee.[4] The liberal Democratic Study Group has found it necessary to exert pressure on the party leaders to secure better committee assignments for liberal Democrats, with some measure of success. The Republican committee on committees would appear to be more representative of the party membership, but it too consists of the most senior members, and the actual assignments are made by a subcommittee consisting of the senior members from the seven or eight states with the largest number of Republican members of the House.

The party leaders in both houses take an active part in committee assignments, consulting with the committee on committees. Immediately after election, new House members usually undertake an active campaign to secure desirable committee assignments, enlisting the aid of older party members from their states. The senior party member from the state, the dean of the delegation, advises the new members and presents their requests and qualifications to the committee on committees, seeking to get the best available assignments for the new members from his state.

CHAIRMEN OF STANDING COMMITTEES

Under the custom of seniority (discussed below), the majority-party member who has the longest continuous service on the committee is invariably elected as chairman. As a rule, he has served for many years in Congress and for nearly as long as a member of the committee, and he is usually of advanced age. Whether or not it is true, it is often stated that Congress is ruled by its elders. The validity of the contention may be indicated by the ages of the chairmen and ranking minority members (who become chairmen when their party is in power) of the most powerful committees of each house. In 1971, the average age of the chairmen of the 10 major committees of the Senate was 66.6 years and that of the ranking minority members was 69.8 years. In the House, the average age of the chairmen of the 10 major committees was 72.1 years and that of the ranking minority-party members was 64.8 years. Three of the chairmen of these com-

---

[4] *Ibid.*, p. 348.

mittees in both houses were more than 80 years old; eight were in their seventies; six were in their sixties; and only two were less than 60 years of age. As pointed out in Chapter 2, the chairmen of the 10 major Senate committees had served an average of 24.7 years in the Senate, and the chairmen of the 10 major House committees had served an average of 33 years in the House![5]

The position of chairman is one of great power and prestige. He directs the work of the committee; appoints the chairmen and members of subcommittees; refers to them the bills that he wants to be considered; and has the leading vote in policy decisions. In some committees, the chairman is ex officio a member of all subcommittees and, when he attends a meeting of a subcommittee, is always invited to preside, which he declines. He appoints the members of the committee staff, except personnel assigned to the opposite party, and directs their activities. Staff members report to him and serve at his pleasure. He calls meetings of the full committee but may refuse to call a meeting if he has reason to believe a majority of the members will take an action that he opposes. The Legislative Reorganization Act of 1946 provides that standing committees shall schedule regular meetings, but not all committees comply with the act. A few standing committees do not utilize subcommittees, which gives the chairmen even greater control over their activities. Members of the majority party who are absent usually give the chairman their proxies, which further increases his power. The 1965 Joint Committee on the Organization of Congress recommended the prohibition of proxy voting in committees, but the 1970 Legislative Reorganization Act merely provided that each committee should decide whether proxy voting shall be used (PL91-510, sec. 106).

When a committee of the House approves a bill, the chairman reports it to the House and seeks a rule from the Rules Committee to make it the order of business. Occasionally, the chairman has refused to report a bill that the committee has approved. In 1965, Rep. Wright Patman, chairman of the House Banking and Currency Committee, failed to call a meeting on the bank merger bill to which he was opposed or to assign it to a subcommittee for hearings. Members of the committee who favored the bill called a meeting of the committee

---

[5] The statistics have been computed from data in *Congressional Quarterly Weekly Report,* vol. 29, no. 3, pp. 126–133, Jan. 15, 1971.

to which Patman was not invited and voted to report the bill. "Although Patman quickly voiced vehement objection to the action, since the House rules allow for the majority to work its will, he had no recourse but to accept the majority's action."[6]

When a bill comes before the House for debate, the chairman manages the floor debate of those in favor of the bill or appoints another member as floor manager. When it is sent to conference between the two houses, the chairman is customarily appointed to the conference committee, and ordinarily he selects the other members.

Some chairmen rule their committees with an iron hand, riding roughshod over the wishes of the members; but other chairmen are more democratic and consult their colleagues. Some committees have definite rules and procedures, but others are run by the chairman as he sees fit. Because of the power, prestige, and permanence of the chairman, and the fact that he is in a position to grant or withhold favors sought by members of the committee, they are reluctant to challenge his actions, however arbitrary. How a former chairman of the House Armed Services Committee, the late Mendel Rivers of South Carolina, ruled his committee is described by Norman C. Miller:

> Lacking seniority, the House doves have great difficulty in airing their views even within committees. Mendel Rivers swiftly retaliates against Armed Services Committee members who cross him; most of the committee members are eager to keep or get military installations in their districts and reflect the pro-Pentagon view in any case.[7]

In a few instances, committee chairmen have been shorn of their powers by a rebellion of the committee, but such action is highly exceptional. The Legislative Reorganization Act of 1970 requires committees to schedule regular meetings, authorizes a majority of the members to call a special meeting if the chairman fails to do so on request of the members, and provides that a bill approved by the committee shall be reported within seven days if so requested by a majority of the members. These provisions are intended to prevent dictatorial chairmen from disregarding the wishes of a majority of the committee, but there is no assurance that they will be observed. Simi-

[6]William L. Morrow, *Congressional Committees,* Charles Scribner's Sons, New York, 1969, p. 134.
[7] *The Wall Street Journal,* July 1, 1970.

lar provisions concerning the operations of committees in the past have at times been disregarded.

Each committee chairman has his own individual style in working with the committee. Some make extensive use of subcommittees to which the chairman delegates broad authority; others make little use of subcommittees and the chairman of the full committee exercises tight control over the subcommittees. A few do not use subcommittees, which permits the chairman to direct all proceedings of the committee. A study of the Senate Banking and Currency Committee from 1953 to 1967 indicates that each of the three chairmen during the period functioned quite differently. In the first two years, when the Republicans were in control, Chairman Homer Capehart of Indiana ran "the committee in a highly centralized manner. Subcommittees existed on paper, but in reality had little power, since major proposals (housing, defense production) were handled in the full committee, where Capehart was personally in charge."[8]

When the Democrats came into power in 1955, Sen. J. William Fulbright of Arkansas, whose principal interest was in foreign relations, became chairman. He delegated the work of the committee largely to its six subcommittees headed by senior Democrats, and permitted the chairmen of the subcommittees to exercise leadership within their assigned jurisdictions, aiding them in securing passage of their legislation. Fulbright was followed by Sen. A. Willis Robertson of Virginia who played a restrained role as chairman, since as a conservative he was not in agreement with a majority of the committee members of his party; but he did not oppose them.

Representative Wilbur D. Mills, Democrat of Arkansas, chairman of the powerful Ways and Means Committee and one of the most influential members of either house, exercises democratic leadership of his committee, working closely with the ranking Republican member, James W. Byrnes of Wisconsin. Mills is noted for hard work, thorough knowledge of complex tax legislation, cooperative relations with members of both parties, and his ability to secure a consensus of the committee, by compromise when necessary, before a bill is reported. He is the swing man of the committee, voting at times with Republi-

[8] John Bibby and Roger Davidson, *On Capitol Hill: Studies in the Legislative Process,* Holt, Rinehart and Winston, Inc., New York, 1967, p. 174. The following account is based on this excellent study.

cans and conservatives on the committee and at other times with liberals. He always makes sure that he has the votes to pass his bills before they are reported, which enhances his power and the prestige of the committee. On tax legislation and social security bills, it is generally conceded that he has greater power than any other member of either house or even the President.[9]

Representative Carl Vinson of Georgia, who had served in Congress for more than 50 years when he retired in 1965, is a good example of the great power wielded by the chairman of a major congressional committee. He served as chairman of the Naval Affairs Committee of the House from 1931 until 1947, when he became chairman of the combined Armed Services Committee, a position that he held, except for two terms when the Republican party was in control, until 1965. Nicknamed the "Admiral," he referred to the Navy as "my Navy." When it was reported that he would be offered the post of Secretary of Defense by President Kennedy in 1961, he is said to have declined, saying that he "would rather run the Pentagon from up here." High-ranking admirals or generals testifying before the committee were addressed as "Boy, what did you say that name was?" Junior members of the committee fared little better.

He ruled his committee with an iron hand, often refusing to permit members of the committee to question witnesses. On one occasion when Lyndon B. Johnson, a member of the committee, attempted to ask a question about a naval base in Texas, Vinson cut him short, saying to the witness, "Admiral, we must get on with other matters." Johnson retorted heatedly, "It looks like after a man has served on the committee for eight years he would be entitled to one question," to which Vinson replied, "All right, but just one."[10]

THE CUSTOM OF SENIORITY

Under the custom of seniority, often referred to as the "rule" of seniority although it is not required by the rules of either house, members of each party are ranked according to their length of continuous service

[9] John F. Manley, "Wilbur D. Mills: A Study of Congressional Influence," *American Political Science Review,* vol. 63, pp. 442–464, 1968.

[10] The above account is taken largely from Richard Bolling, *House Out of Order,* E. P. Dutton & Co., Inc., New York, 1965, pp. 87–90.

in the House or Senate and also according to their length of continuous service on standing committees. As we shall see, seniority on a standing committee is more important than seniority in the House or Senate. The member of the majority party with the longest continuous service on each standing committee automatically becomes chairman of the committee and continues as chairman when his party is in the majority and the voters of his district or state continue to reelect him. Neither the leaders nor the members of his party in Congress have any discretion in the selection of members to serve in the powerful positions of chairmen of standing committees. No other legislative body in the world follows the automatic rule of seniority in selecting its principal officers. The senior minority-party member on each standing committee is known as the "ranking member," and he is the leader of the minority-party members on the committee.

If a member retires from Congress or fails of reelection, he loses his seniority; and, if he is later reelected, he must start at the bottom of the seniority ladder. When Sen. Hubert Humphrey of Minnesota left the Senate in 1965 to become Vice President he ranked number 17 in seniority, but when he returned to the Senate in 1971 he ranked 91, just above the entering class of 1971 because of his prior service. He did not rank high enough to be appointed to one of the most desired committees—Foreign Relations, Appropriations, and Finance—but was appointed to the Agriculture Committee. He was assigned to one of the least desirable office suites in the Old Senate Office Building with old fashioned, long-used office furnishings.

Seniority, writes George Goodwin, Jr., "is more than a means of choosing committee chairmen; it is a means of assigning members to committees, of choosing subcommittee chairmen and conference committee members. It affects the deference shown to legislators on the floor, the assignment of office space, even invitations to dinner."[11] Seniority accords members the right to retain their committee assignments as long as they are reelected, unless they request assignment to another committee. The lowest-ranking party members, however, may lose their committee assignments when the number of committee seats assigned to their party is reduced. Transfers to a preferred committee are usually made on the basis of seniority. Neither commit-

[11] "The Seniority System in Congress," *American Political Science Review,* vol. 53, p. 412, June, 1959.

tee chairmen nor members are subject to being removed from a committee because of refusal to support the position of their party on legislation. They are free to oppose the party that they represent whenever they wish without endangering their committee assignments.[12] A few members have been stripped of their seniority and committee assignments because of openly opposing the presidential candidate of their party but other members have opposed their party's national ticket without incurring any disciplinary action.

The most senior members of the majority party are customarily, but not invariably, appointed as chairmen of the subcommittees, which, next to the committee chairmanships, are the most powerful positions in each house. The chairmen of some subcommittees have greater power and prestige than the chairmen of minor committees. The senior committee members of each party are given the preferred subcommittee assignments, though the committee chairman has some discretion in making the assignments. The ranking committee members are also customarily appointed to the powerful conference committees.

In committee hearings, the senior members of each party are called upon alternately to question witnesses. Junior members are called upon last. As one representative has stated: "The pickings may be a little lean when they get down to the freshman. But, being a politician, he will extract some advantage from the most meager bones."[13] Senior members are called upon first in executive (closed) session to express their view on legislation under consideration, and they take the leading part in the debates when bills come before either house for consideration. Junior members, especially in the House, are expected to be seen but seldom heard. Among the other perquisites of senior members is the choice of office suites when vacancies occur.

The rule of seniority was not strictly followed by the Speaker, who, before 1911, made the committee assignments in the House. At times

---

[12] Representative Adam Clayton Powell, chairman of the House Education and Labor Committee, was removed from the chairmanship of the committee in 1967 by the Democratic party caucus—the first removal of a chairman in more than 50 years—not for opposing the legislative program of his party but for conduct that brought discredit on Congress.

[13] Clem Miller, *Member of the House,* Charles Scribner's Sons, New York, 1962, p. 7.

he dropped members from committees or refused to reappoint a committee chairman. Since 1911, the rule of seniority has become so firmly a part of the traditions of both houses that it will not be easily changed. Several members of Congress testifying before the Joint Committee on the Organization of Congress in 1965 urged that the custom be modified to permit the majority party caucus to elect any one of the three senior members of a standing committee as chairman, but this proposal was not recommended by the committee. Under its terms of reference, the committee was precluded from making any recommendations for changes in the rules, traditions, and practices of Congress, a restriction undoubtedly intended to prevent any recommendation touching upon seniority.

Many younger members of Congress are critical of the custom of seniority, the effect of which is to place control of each house in the hands of its elders and in large measure to deprive junior members of the opportunity to influence legislative policies and to render distinguished service until they have acquired seniority. The rule of seniority is discouraging to new members of Congress, especially of the House, where they often have to serve several terms before securing a desirable committee assignment. Senior committee members expect junior members to listen and learn rather than to express their own views. "As a member rises in rank on a committee," states the *Congressional Quarterly Weekly Report,* "his chances increase of being heard, of asking witnesses questions, and of handling major legislation."[14] Gerald Clarke, writing in *Time,* states: "In the House, where the seniority system is most oppressive, a new member is virtually impotent. Whatever his talent or promise, he must resign himself to a marginal role in Congress for the first few terms." Charles Frankel, Assistant Secretary of State from 1965 to 1967, expressed the same view: "Young bright congressmen come to Washington full of ideas and interest, and shortly become discouraged."[15]

Senior members defend the rule of seniority, which makes advancement automatic for members who continue to be reelected and gives them relative independence from control or discipline by the party leaders. The seniority system, it should be noted, can also be frustrat-

[14] Vol. 39, no. 3, p. 134, Jan. 15, 1971.
[15] Quoted by Clarke in *Time,* Dec. 14, 1970.

ing to senior members. There are few things more frustrating than to rank third or fourth on standing committees of Congress at the age of 70, knowing that the coveted prize of committee chairman will not be attained, if at all, until one is too old to derive much satisfaction from it. Not only are the chairmen of the standing committees usually of advanced age, but the next several highest ranking members are also usually from 65 to 70 years of age. Mendel Rivers of South Carolina, who died near the end of the Ninety-first Congress in December, 1970, was succeeded as chairman of the House Armed Services Committee by Rep. F. Edward Hébert of Louisiana, who was 70 years of age and had served in Congress for 30 years. Senator Richard Russell of Georgia, chairman of the Senate Appropriations Committee, died shortly after the opening of Congress in 1971, having served in the Senate for 38 years. He was succeeded by Sen. Allen J. Ellender of Louisiana, 81 years of age, who had served in the Senate for 34 years.

The major criticism of the rule or custom of seniority, sometimes called the "rule of senility," is that it elevates to the powerful committee chairmanships persons of advanced age who are unable to provide vigorous, effective leadership and prevents the appointment of younger and more able persons. One of the most trenchant criticisms of the custom of seniority in filling the committee chairmanships was written by Mayor John V. Lindsay of New York when he was a member of the House, as follows:

> As presently practiced, the system is unsound, inflexible, undemocratic, and certainly discouraging to junior members of Congress. Even the "law of the jungle" operates on a higher level than the "law" of seniority; the first works to assure the survival of the fittest; the latter operates only to assure the survival of the oldest.[16]

Another objection to the inflexible custom of seniority is that it deprives the party leadership of any voice in the selection of committee chairmen, and often elevates members who are strongly opposed to the party policies and programs to the powerful positions of committee chairmen. It is not uncommon for committee chairmen to use their

[16] House Republican Task Force on Congressional Reform, *We Propose: A Modern Congress,* ed. Mary McInnis, McGraw-Hill Book Company, New York, 1966, p. 26.

power to block programs to which their party is pledged in its platform. Committee chairmen are not responsible to the congressional party or subject to its discipline. Their only responsibility is to the voters of their state or district who elected them and can vote them out of office.

Most committee chairmen come from safe, often one-party districts or states, otherwise they would not have acquired the seniority that elevated them to be chairmen. After they have become chairmen, with the added prestige, power, and ability to secure benefits for their districts, they become even more unbeatable and consequently more independent of national and congressional party leadership. "The committee chairmen," writes Ralph K. Huitt, "especially when they are clothed with the immunity of a seniority rule, are chieftains to be bargained with, not lieutenants to be commanded." [17] In his study of the Senate, Donald R. Matthews discovered that the party-loyalty scores in the voting of 21 committee chairmen declined after they became chairmen; 2 remained the same; and 4 increased. The last 4 were all "moderate" Republicans who became chairmen as Eisenhower entered the White House. [18]

The rule of seniority in the selection of chairmen of committees is defended on the ground that it works reasonably well, and no better alternative system has been proposed. Senator Hugh Scott of Pennsylvania, testifying before the Joint Committee on the Organization of Congress in 1965, maintained that it would be undesirable to elect committee chairmen, which would "turn over the chairmanship to a popularity contest" and result in "incessant lobbying day to day among the members of the committee for the opportunity to succeed to the chairmanship." [19] Representative Emanuel Celler of New York, chairman of the Judiciary Committee, who has served 48 years in Congress, said:

> The seniority system, while it may produce here and there an inadequate chairman, on the whole has produced competent and capable chairmen

[17] "Democratic Party Leadership in the Senate," *American Political Science Review*, vol. 55, p. 335, 1961.

[18] *U.S. Senators and Their World*, p. 164.

[19] *Hearings*, p. 301.

familiar with the subject matter before it, familiar with the rules of the House, familiar with the management of a bill, in a way no other member can be.[20]

One unfortunate effect of the seniority rule is to give the 12 Southern states, which have approximately 25 percent of the seats in each house, a majority of the chairmanships in each house when the Democrats are in control and a majority to the Middle West when the Republicans control Congress. The concentration of power in Southern members when the Democrats are in control of Congress, as they have been during 34 of the past 38 years, is one of the most significant aspects of Congress, leading William S. White in his study of the Senate to refer to it as a "Southern Institution."[21] Southern control is no less operative in the House than in the Senate and in both houses is due not only to the number of chairmanships held by the South but also to the preponderant number of senior Southern members on the major committees. In the eight years when the Democrats were in control of Congress from 1947 through 1958, 62 percent of the House committee chairmen and 53 percent of the Senate chairmen were from the South. During the four years when the Republicans were in control, 66 percent of the House chairmen and 53 percent of the Senate chairmen were from the Middle West.[22] A large proportion of the Democratic chairmen came from rural areas of the South, and many of the Republican chairmen came from rural areas of the Middle West.

The dominance of Southern members was even greater over the most powerful committees. Minor committees in each house have far less power than the major committees, and most members of these committees seek a transfer to a more desirable committee as soon as they have sufficient seniority. Only members from safe seats are ordinarily transferred to the House Appropriations Committee and certain other top committees. In 1971, 8 of the 10 chairmen of major commit-

[20] *Ibid.,* p. 698.

[21] *Citadel: The Story of the U.S. Senate,* Harper & Row, Publishers, Incorporated, New York, 1956, p. 68.

[22] George Goodwin, Jr., "The Seniority System," *American Political Science Review,* vol. 53, pp. 412–436, 1959.

tees of the Senate were from the South; in the House 6 of the 10 chairmen of the major committees, including the three most powerful committees—Rules, Ways and Means, and Appropriations—were from the South. A majority of the chairmen of the subcommittees of these major committees in each house were also from the South. When a Democratic Southern chairman dies or retires, his place is usually taken by another Southern Democrat.

Why does the South capture a majority of the powerful chairmanships in each house when the Democrats are in control, and the Middle West when the Republicans are in the majority? Several hypotheses may be advanced. The South has long been solidly Democratic, especially in the election of congressmen and state and local officials; and many areas of the Middle West outside of metropolitan centers have been solidly Republican over a long period of time. In one-party areas of the South, a Democratic nominee usually faces no opposition or only token opposition in the general election; and, with the advantages of incumbency, which for a congressman are very great, he is rarely defeated in the primary of his own party. This is also true of the strong Republican areas of the Middle West, but perhaps not to the same extent as in the South. In most other areas of the country, there have been sweeping changes in party preference, especially following the Great Depression of the 1930s. Many congressional districts that were once safely Republican are today safely Democratic. Members of Congress with the highest seniority come from districts or states that have been safe for the same party over long periods.

Another reason for the dominance of the South when the Democrats are in control is that many of its districts appear to have a tradition of electing young members to Congress when vacancies occur and reelecting them continuously until they achieve a high seniority ranking. One from a safe district who enters Congress before he is 40 years of age may reasonably expect to become chairman of a committee, but those who are over 40 upon entering have considerably less chance, and those who are over 50 have almost no chance at all.

Little defense can be made of a system that elevates members to the powerful positions of committee chairmen solely because they have served longest on the committee, without taking into account their abilities, qualities of leadership, physical stamina, and whether they support the policies of the party. The work of Congress is too important today, the responsibilities of its committee chairmen are too demanding, and the need for effective committee leadership is too great for Congress to forego any choice in selecting committee chairmen by continuing the inflexible rule of seniority. No other responsible governing body, public or private, makes seniority the sole criterion in selecting its principal officers. The rule of seniority has not provided the effective, vigorous committee leadership that the nation needs. Although there have been some able chairman of advanced age and others who were adequate if not distinguished, there have also been chairmen of committees of great importance to the country who were inadequate, ineffective, and unable to provide needed leadership. And there have been those out of sympathy with the policies of their party who have used their power to block needed legislation.

The only defense of the rule of seniority is the contention that the election of committee chairmen would lead to unseemly contests, and that appointment by the party leader in Congress would place too much power in the hands of one man. These are not the only alternative methods to the rule of seniority. The use of a committee on committees, as at present, subject to effective control by the party membership in caucus, which both parties in the House adopted in 1971, is a suitable method of electing committee chairmen, provided the party leadership, with the support of the members of the party, uses this procedure to select qualified chairmen and to oust recalcitrant or ineffective chairmen. Only time will tell whether the party leaders will have the courage to break with tradition and make effective use of this procedure. There will doubtless be strong resistance by senior members to any modification of the rule of seniority and changes will not come easily.

In 1970, a group of younger members of each party in the House led a movement against the rule of seniority and urged other reforms of Congress. Each party caucus appointed a caucus committee to make recommendations. Each of these party committees recommended that the rule of seniority should not be inflexibly followed and that other considerations should also be taken into account in the selection of committee chairmen. To carry out this recommendation it was proposed that the caucus rules be amended to permit a number of members to challenge the selection of a chairman or other members of a committee and thus require the selection to be put to a vote of the caucus. If defeated by a majority vote, the committee on committees would be required to bring in another selection. Both parties adopted the proposed change in the rules. A group of liberal Democrats challenged the selection of Rep. John McMillan of South Carolina as chairman of the District of Columbia Committee, a post that he had held for more than 20 years. McMillan was unpopular in the House and had been described as a man who had "singlehanded held the District of Columbia in bondage," but he won reelection by a vote of 126 to 96. In the debate, Rep. Wilbur D. Mills of Arkansas, one of the most powerful members of the House, said that if McMillan were defeated, no chairman or member would be secure in his committee assignment, but could be unseated by the caucus.[23] This was the purpose of the change in the rules—to make committee chairmen and members more responsible to the party membership. No challenges were made in the Republican caucus.

SELECT AND JOINT COMMITTEES

In addition to standing committees, each house appoints select committees from time to time, principally to conduct inquiries. Select committees, in contrast to standing committees, exist only during the Congress that established them, though they may be continued by the following Congress. They are not given authority to report legislation to the parent body, but only to make studies and investigations and make reports of their findings and conclusions. In the Ninety-first Congress (1969–1971) the Senate created select committees on Nutrition and Human Needs, Small Business, the Aging, and Standards and Conduct; the House created select committees on Small Business and Crime.

Congress also utilizes a number of joint committees and commissions, the two most important of which are the Joint Committee on Atomic Energy, the only joint committee that is authorized to report legislation, and the Joint Economic Committee, which reviews the President's Economic Reports, conducts hearings and studies of the national economy, and submits reports on economic policies to Congress. Congress appoints temporary joint committees to conduct in-

[23] *The Wall Street Journal,* Jan. 27, 1971.

quiries; for example, the Joint Committee on the Organization of Congress was created in 1965. It is often proposed that Congress should make greater use of joint legislative committees to facilitate consideration of legislation. Joint committees are successfully used by a number of state legislatures but have found little favor in Congress because each house is jealous of its prerogatives, and it is believed that joint committees would be contrary to the bicameral principle.

SUBCOMMITTEES

The detailed consideration of proposed bills and appropriations today is performed ordinarily not by the standing committees but by subcommittees.[24] Each Congress utilizes about 250 subcommittees. Some are standing subcommittees that continue from one session to another; some are created for one session only; some are assigned a definite area of legislation, but others are numbered committees without definite assignments; some are ad hoc, created to consider particular bills. A few standing committees (for example, Ways and Means, and Internal Security in the House, and the Senate Finance Committee) do not use subcommittees. Many subcommittees have their own staffs, separate budgets, committee offices and hearing rooms, and function very much like standing committees, though their bills and reports must be approved by the full committee before they are submitted to the House or Senate. Other subcommittees have less autonomy. The chairman of an important subcommittee, especially Appropriations subcommittees, wields greater power and has greater prestige than the chairmen of minor standing committees.

A typical legislative committee of either house has from 8 to 10 subcommittees, each assigned a definite area of legislation. The Senate committee on Labor and Public Welfare, for example, has eight standing subcommittees on Health, Education, Labor, Veterans' Affairs, Railroad Retirement, Migratory Labor, Manpower, and Poverty and six special subcommittees. Most subcommittees are primarily concerned with the consideration of proposed legislation, but they also

[24] See George Goodwin, Jr., "Subcommittees: The Miniature Legislatures of Congress," *American Political Science Review*, vol. 56, pp. 596–604, 1962.

conduct investigations, and a few have been created for the sole purpose of conducting investigations.

Subcommittees are subject to varying degrees of control by the parent committee, whose approval is required before a bill can be reported to the House or Senate. The chairman of the parent committee may exercise detailed control over subcommittees; he appoints the chairmen and members, assigns bills for their consideration, and in some cases assigns the staff to serve the subcommittee and controls its expenditures. He ordinarily consults with the ranking minority-party member before making minority-party appointments to subcommittees. The rule of seniority is usually but not always followed in appointments to subcommittees, which permits the chairman some discretion. With rare exception, however, the highest-ranking party members are appointed as chairmen of subcommittees. Some committee chairmen exercise tight control over subcommittees, but others do not. A congressional staff member observed: "Given an active subcommittee chairman working in a specialized field with a staff of his own, the parent committee can do no more than change the grammar of a subcommittee report."[25] The appropriations subcommittees in both houses, for example, strongly resist any changes in their recommendations, pointing out that other members of the full committee have not attended the extended hearings on the department budgets and consequently are not qualified to second-guess the decisions of the subcommittee.

The use of subcommittees has relieved the standing committees of much of the time-consuming work of conducting extended hearings and giving detailed consideration to proposed legislation. It has also permitted greater specialization of labor among committee members. Even more important, it has permitted the sharing of power, prestige, and responsibilities of the chairman with the senior members of the full committee who serve as subcommittee chairmen, many of whom are frustrated by the lack of responsibilities before being appointed as subcommittee chairmen. Although they are not young men, they are at least younger, as a rule, than the chairman of the full committee. Subcommittees have also provided increased opportunities for

[25] *Ibid.,* p. 596.

younger members to participate actively in committee work, and, to some extent, have corrected the weaknesses of the committee system. On the other hand, the trend is to extend the seniority rule to subcommittees and to encourage the enactment of legislation dealing with details that should be left to the responsible executive officers. In the hearings of the Joint Committee on the Organization of Congress, Rep. Chet Holifield of California warned that by too much specialization of labor and proliferation of subcommittees "we defeat our own purposes." [26]

It may be questioned whether the proliferation of subcommittees and their increasing role is wholly desirable, but because of the greatly increased work load of Congress it is doubtless unavoidable. It has resulted in greater specialization and division of responsibility for legislative policies by creating additional centers of power. The increased use of subcommittees has resulted in a heavy work load for members of the Senate, many of whom serve on 10 or more subcommittees, in addition to their committee assignments. Senate subcommittee meetings are usually poorly attended, partly because of the conflicts with other scheduled meetings. Subcommittee chairmen often have difficulty in rounding up one or two other members to attend scheduled hearings. Senator Dirksen once complained that he would have to have roller skates to put in an appearance at the meetings of the 15 subcommittees of which he was a member and could not possibly keep fully informed about their work. Members of the House, being much more numerous, have fewer subcommittee assignments and are not similarly burdened by subcommittee work.

COMMITTEE STAFFS [27]

Before 1946, congressional committees were poorly staffed to deal with the increasingly complex legislative problems. The typical committee had a small clerical staff consisting of one to three male employees who held the title of clerk and several stenographic and

---

[26] *Hearings,* p. 195.

[27] See Kenneth Kofmehl, *Professional Staffs of Congress,* Purdue University Studies, Lafayette, Ind., 1962. The author has drawn heavily in this section on this excellent study.

clerical women employees. The maximum salary paid, with a few exceptions, was $3,500 annually. Employees were appointed by the chairman of the committee and could be fired by him at any time for any reason or no reason at all. Usually they were residents of the chairman's state or district and were patronage appointees of the chairman.

One of the most important features of the Legislative Reorganization Act of 1946 was to authorize each standing committee to appoint four professional staff members in addition to its clerical staff. No limit was placed on the number of professional staff members of the Appropriations committees. In addition, the act removed the previous salary limitation, which had handicapped committee chairmen in recruiting qualified persons. The recommendation for the creation of a nonpartisan, professional, permanent staff, selected on the basis of qualifications, under a congressional merit system, was defeated because of the opposition of some committee chairmen who had always regarded committee staff appointments as personal patronage.

Since 1946, the standing committees' staffs have greatly increased in size and, fortunately, also in qualifications. Many of the senior professional staff members are paid salaries today ranging from $20,000 to $35,000. Many are professionally trained and specially qualified by reason of previous experience, but others are political appointees with limited qualifications. Some chairmen make a practice of recruiting new staff members from executive departments, thus securing the services of persons who are already well versed in the subject matter with which the committee deals. Although staff members have no security of tenure, many committees follow the practice of retaining experienced staff members when there is a change in party control or committee chairman.

It is not unusual today for a congressional committee to have 20 or more staff members, including temporary personnel engaged in special investigations. A few committees have staffs of 50 or more persons. Many subcommittees have separate staffs of several professional and clerical employees. Committee staff members are not under civil service but are appointed by the chairman, subject to the approval of the committee. Methods of recruitment and selection of staff members vary widely. They may be selected (1) by the chairman, (2) by the chairman in consultation with the ranking minority-party member, (3) partly by the chairman and partly by other members of the committee, (4) by a committee on staffing, (5) by the director of the staff. In all cases the appointment is made by the chairman. Methods 4 and 5 would appear to be best suited to securing qualified personnel, but any of the methods will work satisfactorily if the need for qualified and preferably nonpartisan staff members is recognized. Although some patronage appointments are still made, Kofmehl reports that by and large the committees have increasingly made an effort to select competent personnel on the basis of merit without regard to party affiliation.

A competent, professionally trained, highly qualified, and preferably nonpartisan staff is essential today to the work of congressional committees. The executive departments have become too big, too complex, and too technical in their various activities for members of congressional committees to form intelligent judgments about the decisions that they are called upon to make and legislation that they pass upon without the assistance of a competent staff. Under the direction of the chairman of the committee or subcommittee, the staff assists the committee in a variety of ways: it arranges for the hearings, collects information required to pass upon legislative policies and prepares it in a form that busy members can readily use, conducts research studies on the instruction of the chairman, prepares drafts of legislation, writes the first draft of the committee reports on legislation, and renders other assistance desired by the committee. The typical staff member is not an expert, but rather a generalist who is exceedingly well informed on the subject with which the committee is concerned and knows where to turn to secure detailed information. According to Kofmehl:

> A committee staff member must be fundamentally a generalist. A committee considers such a diversity of subjects that he could not possibly be a specialist in more than a fraction of them. Even if he were an expert on some aspects of the committee work, he would have to justify his continued existence on the staff by functioning as a generalist in other areas. The changing emphases of congressional attention and the small size of the staff would require him to deal with multiple matters outside of his specialty. ... It is the broad-gauged individual with an active intellectual

curiosity, ability to see inter-relationships, quick apperceptiveness, and mental agility who best fulfills that role.[28]

A committee staff aide must be flexible so that he can shift from one assignment to another as the work or emphasis of the committee changes. He must be able to serve not only the chairman to whom he is directly responsible but also other members of the committee and to command their confidence and respect, irrespective of whether he agrees with their points of view. He must be articulate and able to express himself clearly and succinctly, whether in speaking or writing, but must be reserved in expressing his own opinions, realizing that his function is to aid the committee in securing the facts that it needs to reach decisions rather than to express his own opinions. He should avoid taking sides on issues before the committee and above all should not become a crusader for one side of an issue. He should have a clear conception of the functions of a staff aide. If there are important facts that he thinks should be called to the attention of the committee, instead of speaking out, he should, as a rule, speak privately to the chairman.

The successful staff aide becomes thoroughly informed about legislation within the jurisdiction of the committee, its background, and the administration of the executive departments and agencies concerned. He should be able to work cooperatively with his opposite number in executive departments and to establish relations that will enable him to secure from them the information needed by the committee.[29]

The professional staffs have greatly strengthened the work of standing committees. Although the size of the professional staffs has greatly increased since 1946, some congressmen urge that the committees should have much larger staffs of professional and expert personnel. They contend that the committees cannot trust the testi-

---

[28] *Ibid.,* pp. 88–89.

[29] Mark Sheilds, former distinguished clerk of the House Appropriations Committee, was held in the highest esteem, not only by the members of the Committee, but also by the chief administrative officers of the executive departments. Members of the committee related to the author that he was of great value to them because he could secure needed information from the department officers who trusted him.

mony of departmental officials and experts, which invariably supports the requests of the departments and is self-serving, hence the committees need their own staffs of experts to advise and inform them.

Concerning the tendency to increase the size of congressional professional staffs, Kofmehl has warned against the dangers of overstaffing:

> Having become persuaded of the utility of professional aides, Congress like many a religious convert threatens to become overzealous. . . . There is a growing tendency to regard staffing as a panacea. If Congress only had a larger staff, they assert, it could legislate in detailed instead of broad terms and halt the trend toward delegation of increasing amounts of authority to the administrative establishment. With enough staff, they believe, Congress could exercise minute supervision of the executive branch and really make its weight felt. Many of these are highly dubious propositions both as to ends and means. If a little staffing is good, it does not necessarily follow that a whole lot more is better.[30]

Representative Holifield of California expressed similar views in his testimony before the Joint Committee on the Organization of Congress in 1965:

> The emphasis we should give to committee staffing, it seems to me, is improvement in quality rather than mere increase in numbers. After all, we do not want to build an unwieldly congressional bureaucracy. The Congress will be best served if its professional staffs remain moderate in numbers, high in competence, broad in understanding, versatile and flexible in adaptation, and nonpartisan in outlook. In staffing, emphasis should be on better rather than more.[31]

Most of the standing committees of Congress prefer to have a relatively small staff of generalists in whom they have confidence and with whom they can work closely, rather than to have a large staff. It is questionable whether congressional committees should have their own staffs of experts to advise them, although they are free to call in

---

[30] Kofmehl, *Professional Staffs of Congress,* p. 5.

[31] *Hearings,* p. 196.

outside experts when there is need. Congress should not become bogged down in a morass of technical details. Each branch of the government and each level of authority should operate at its own level, make only the decisions that are appropriate to it.

In recent years, Republican members have complained that they are not adequately served by the standing committee staffs, and urge that the minority party should be provided with special staffs to serve them. The 1970 Legislative Reorganization Act provided that the professional staff of each standing committee should be increased from four to six members; and, if requested by the minority members, two of the professional staff and one clerical employee should be assigned to them and should be selected by the minority members. The provision, however, was stricken in the House on the motion of Representative Holifield, who had previously raised the issue in the Democratic caucus and secured a vote that bound Democratic members to vote for the motion. It should be noted that in all but one or two committees of each house the minority party is regularly allocated one or more staff members by the chairman. Those who oppose a statutory provision creating separate party staff for each committee fear that it might lead to increased partisanship and feel that a nonpartisan staff to serve all members is preferable.

In addition to the regular committee staff, several committees in each house that carry on large-scale investigations have large temporary staffs whose salaries are paid out of special funds voted for the purpose. A few committees have contracted with private research organizations and universities to conduct research studies. Each house of Congress has an office of legislative counsel, whose function is to draft bills at the request of committees or members. These offices are noted for their highly expert and nonpartisan staffs, who assist the committee staffs, many of whom are attorneys, in the highly technical work of preparing legislation.

GENERAL ACCOUNTING OFFICE

The General Accounting Office (GAO), which is regarded as an agency of Congress, renders various and extensive services to congressional committees and members. The statutes provide it to furnish staff aides to committees on request. In fiscal year 1969, 68 professional staff members of the GAO were on loan to standing committees of Congress at a total cost of $416,375.[32] In addition, it conducted 92 special audits, investigations, and management studies at the request of Congress and its committees. It is frequently called upon by congressional committees for reports on proposed bills, for testimony before committees, and for assistance in congressional investigations. Although estimates of the total cost of services rendered to Congress by the General Accounting Office are not available, it probably amounts to several million dollars annually.

CONGRESSIONAL RESEARCH SERVICE

The Legislative Reference Service of the Library of Congress, which preceded the Congressional Research Service, dates from 1914. It was a relatively small reference service; in 1944 it had a budget of $145,000 and employed a small staff of librarians and subject specialists in the intermediate grades. The Legislative Reorganization Act of 1946 made the Service a separate department in the Library of Congress, expanded its functions to include research and consulting, and authorized the appointment of senior specialists in a score of broad legislative fields at annual salaries of about $8,000. By 1955, the staff had expanded to include 130 lawyers, economists, political scientists, historians, librarians, and analysts, and the budget had increased to approximately 1 million dollars.[33] By 1965, the staff had nearly doubled and the annual budget was approximately 2 million dollars.

The Legislative Reorganization Act of 1970 expanded the functions of the Service, made it practically autonomous, although it remains in the Library of Congress, and placed the Service directly under the

---

[32] *Annual Report of the Comptroller General of the United States, 1969,* Appendix H-7, p. 384.

[33] See George B. Galloway, *Congressional Reorganization Revisited,* Bureau of Government Research, University of Maryland, College Park, 1956, p. 5; Kofmehl, *Professional Staffs of Congress, passim.*

supervision of the Joint Committee on the Library of Congress. Its name was changed to the Congressional Research Service to emphasize that its primary function is to serve as a research arm of Congress instead of being a reference service. "Members misuse the Service," said Chairman Mike Monroney during the hearings of the Joint Committee on the Organization of Congress, "to help them answer constituent mail. . . . Congress must be willing to give up the service for high school students [aiding them in writing term papers] . . . or we will have to set up another research pool outside of the Library of Congress."[34]

To perform its expanded functions, the Service is authorized to employ an unspecified number of specialists and senior specialists in each of 22 fields, ranging from agriculture to veterans' affairs, and in such other fields as the director may consider appropriate. They are exempt from civil service and, to assure adequate salaries to attract highly qualified persons, the act provides that the grade of senior specialist shall not be paid less than the salary paid the highest grade in the executive branch for positions with corresponding responsibilities. The act also authorizes placing the positions of specialists and senior specialists, with the approval of the Joint Committee on the Library, in one of the supergrades with salaries of up to about $35,000. No limit is placed on the number of supergrade positions in the Service, although the number in executive departments is limited by law and the approval of the Civil Service Commission is required before a position may be placed in a supergrade.

The Service will doubtless be expanded within the next few years and will probably be one of the highest-paid professional staffs in the government. Whether it will become, as intended by the act, an effective research agency to serve Congress and its committees is uncertain. The specialists in the Legislative Reference Service in past years have usually been isolated from firsthand contacts with the members and staff aides of committees whom they serve and have not always been effectively utilized.[35]

---

[34] Hearings, p. 303.
[35] See Kofmehl, Professional Staffs of Congress, p. 10.

CONFERENCE COMMITTEES

Congress makes extensive use of conference committees to reconcile the differences in bills that have been passed by both houses.[36] Identical bills must be passed by each house before they are signed by the presiding officers and sent to the President for his approval. It is unusual for an important bill to be passed initially in identical form by both houses. Unless the house that first passed the bill accepts the amendments of the second house, it is ordinarily sent to a conference committee to compromise the differences and to reach an agreement upon an identical bill that is reported to both houses for approval.

When both houses agree to send a bill to conference, the presiding officer of each house appoints the members of the conference committee, or "managers" as they are called, on the recommendation of the chairman of the committee that reported the bill. By custom the chairman names himself and the ranking committee members of each party and may name two or more additional senior committee members. If the bill was proposed by a subcommittee, ordinarily the chairman and a ranking minority member of the subcommittee are named to serve on the conference committee. Each house has one vote in the conference committee, regardless of the number of members appointed to the conference committee.

Conference committees enjoy such great powers in the revision of bills that they are sometimes referred to as the "third house" of Congress. Under the rules of each house, the conference committee must not alter or delete provisions that have been passed in identical form by both houses or write into the bill provisions that have not been passed by either house, but it may make "a germane modification of the subjects in disagreement."[37] Its function is to seek a middle ground when there are differences in the bill as passed by the two houses, but in practice the conference committee often substantially revises the bill. If the second house has revised the bill by striking everything after the enacting clause, as sometimes occurs, the conference committee has a relatively free hand in rewriting the bill. The

[36] See Gilbert Y. Steiner, *The Congressional Conference Committee,* The University of Illinois Press, Urbana, 1951.

[37] Legislative Reorganization Act of 1946, section 135.

senior committee members, who know in advance that they will serve on the conference committee, may see to it that the bill contains provisions for "trading purposes" when it goes to conference.

Conference committees meet in closed sessions. Despite rules designed to limit the changes that they may make in bills passed by both houses, they often rewrite bills, and their revision becomes law because it is very difficult to defeat a bill that has been agreed to by the conferees of both houses. Senator George Norris criticized the great power vested in a few senior members of the conference committee:

> This conference committee is many times, in very important matters of legislation, the most important branch of our legislature. There is no record kept of the workings of the conference committee. Its work is performed, in the main, in secret. ... As a practical proposition, we have legislation, then, not by the voice of the members of Congress but ... by the voice of five or six men.[38]

Similar views were expressed by Rep. Clem Miller:

> [Although] a conference is supposed to be a *resolution* of differences, the finished product is frequently a strange melange of the original ingredients plus others not so easily identified. ... The conference committee is the ultimate flowering of the power of seniority. It is the central core of the power.[39]

In 1948, Sen. William Fulbright satirically congratulated the conferees on a national defense appropriation bill passed in a special session

> ... for so forthrightly disregarding the wishes of the common lay member of the Senate and House. ... There was no need for the ordinary lay members of Congress to come back to Washington for a special session. ... All that is necessary is to reconvene, preferably in secret, only those

---

[38] Quoted by George B. Galloway, *The Legislative Process in Congress,* Thomas Y. Crowell Company, New York, 1953, p. 321.

[39] *Member of the House,* p. 114.

incomparable sages, the conferees of the Appropriations Committee. . . . It is quite clear that regardless of what the common members of this party may wish, the conferees make the decisions.[40]

Bills passed by the House are subject to a rule prohibiting unrelated or non-germane provisions, but the Senate has no germane rule and often adds wholly unrelated provisions to a bill already passed by the House. This device is ordinarily used to speed up enactment. For example, in 1970 the Senate tacked on a popular provision to increase social security payments to a House bill dealing with import quotas in order to make the bill difficult for the President to veto. When the import quota bill was tied up by a filibuster in the Senate, the social security increase was then added as an amendment to another bill that the House had passed, and in this form it was quickly passed by both houses. In this instance, there was no objection in the House, for the Ways and Means Committee had already approved an increase in social security payments, but the House often objects strenuously to nongermane provisions added by the Senate, because they short-circuit committee consideration in the House. The Legislative Reorganization Act of 1970 attempted to make it more difficult to pass a nongermane provision in the House by providing that such a provision is subject to a point of order, which, if accepted by the House, requires a two-thirds vote to pass the nongermane provision.

The managers of each house are required by the rules to fight for the provisions adopted by the house that they represent, though in fact they may have opposed key provisions in disagreement. In such cases they are often accused of yielding to the other house without making a fight. Conferees may be instructed not to yield on certain points, and at times such instructions may be sought by the conferees to strengthen their hands, but each house is aware that compromise is essential to reach an agreement and usually does not tie the hands of its managers.

The conference committee meets behind closed doors under a strict custom that what occurs shall not be revealed outside. A great deal of horse trading goes on, each side yielding on certain points that it does

[40] *Congressional Record,* June 19, 1948, p. 9206. Quoted in Galloway, *The Legislative Process in Congress,* p. 321.

not regard as crucial in exchange for concessions by the other side. Differences in appropriations bills are often compromised by agreeing to a figure midway between the amounts voted by each house. When an agreement has been reached, it is reported to each house, which must accept or reject it without revision. Usually it is accepted, for at this stage it is a choice between accepting the compromise or no bill at all. Most conference committee reports come up in the closing days of the session when members are anxious for Congress to adjourn and are prepared to accept a half loaf rather than no bread at all.

REVIEW QUESTIONS

1. Describe the functions and powers of standing congressional committees. Why are they sometimes referred to as "little legislatures"?

2. Describe how committee assignments in each house are made.

3. What are the powers of committee chairmen? What abuses of their powers led the Joint Committee on the Organization of Congress in 1966 to recommend a committee "bill of rights"?

4. Discuss the custom of seniority, reviewing and commenting on the arguments pro and con.

5. What changes in the custom were made in the House in 1971 and with what results?

6. What is the difference between a standing committee and a select committee?

7. Describe the typical staff of a congressional committee and their functions.

8. What are the functions of conference committees? Why are they sometimes referred to as the "third house"?

5 THE LEGISLATIVE PROCESS

THE ORIGIN OF BILLS

Few of the fourteen thousand bills introduced in each session of Congress are the brainchildren of its members. The majority are initiated by the executive departments, private organizations, or individual citizens. A few are proposed by the President as a part of his legislative program. It is easy to have a bill introduced, but very difficult to secure its enactment. There is no limit on the number of bills that members of Congress may introduce. Members often introduce bills at the request of constituents or others without any intention of pressing for enactment, at times marking such bills to indicate that they were introduced "by request." Thereafter it is up to the initiating group to drum up support and seek a committee hearing on their bill. Only about a thousand bills are passed by each Congress; the vast majority never emerge from the "dim dungeons of silence" of the committee to which they are assigned.

Public bills relate to public affairs, while *private bills* affect only named persons. The latter are used mostly to pay claims of citizens against the government that are not legally allowable in the court of claims. *Joint resolutions,* which have the same effect as statutes, are used for actions of a nonpermanent character. Public bills, which are by far the most important, vary greatly in scope and importance. Most bills amend existing statutes, but others propose new legislation. The large majority are noncontroversial and those that reach the floor are passed without opposition. Usually less than two dozen bills of major importance are taken up in each session of Congress.

LEGISLATIVE PROGRAM OF THE EXECUTIVE Congress increasingly looks to the President to submit a legislative program and devotes most of its attention to his proposals. Formerly, protocol limited the President to general recommendations of policy, leaving the drafting of bills to members of Congress. Jealous of its prerogatives, Congress once returned a petty bill submitted by President Lincoln with a request that it be passed, declining even to consider it. Formerly, bills to carry out the President's recommendations were bootlegged to friendly members of Congress to be introduced as their own, without indicating the source, but today Congress expects the President or the department primarily concerned to submit draft bills to carry out his recommendations. The administration bills are freely revised by Congress and often the final acts bear little resemblance to the original drafts.

Each executive department normally submits to Congress at each session a number of legislative requests, the most important of which may be included in the President's legislative program. The President must be careful, however, not to support too many measures, which would lessen the effect of his endorsements and weaken his role as legislative leader.

One of the most important responsibilities of executive departments is to recommend needed legislation relating to the functions assigned to them. Most of their legislative requests are designed to improve administrative operations, but they also recommend legislation authorizing new policies and programs. The departments are usually well equipped to make recommendations on needed legislation relating to their assigned functions, for their officers are well informed about problems, operations, and public needs and are able to draw upon the technical and legal staff in preparing bills. Department officials, however, must guard against becoming too zealous in advocating proposed legislation, or they will be criticized for lobbying. A 1919 statute prohibits departments from attempting to influence legislation, and, although the statute is not enforced, it acts as a restraint on their legislative activities.

During the preparation of bills, departmental officials usually consult with various interested organizations and congressional leaders, as well as with other executive departments that may be concerned. At this stage compromises and revisions are often made that will greatly facilitate the passage of the bill. If an agreement is not reached, proposed legislation is almost certain to be opposed and will likely be defeated or greatly revised by Congress.

Departmental bills must be "cleared" by the Legislative Reference Division of the Bureau of the Budget to make sure that they are in conformity with the President's program and policies and to assure that other interested departments have been consulted. Many department bills affect other departments in one way or another. Advance consultation permits any differences of opinion to be reconciled before submission of a bill and thus avoids interdepartmental fights before congressional committees. Legislation of major interest to several departments is often prepared under the direction of an interdepartmental committee.[1]

Although in most other countries it is the practice for all important legislation to be proposed by the executive departments, individual members of Congress play an important though a declining role in the initiation of legislation. Many major laws are first proposed by members of Congress, and, after they acquire widespread support, are included in the President's legislative program. Thus, Sen. George Norris advocated a public power program in the Tennessee Valley for

[1] Richard E. Neustadt, "The Presidency and Legislation: The Growth of Central Clearance," *American Political Science Review*, vol. 47, pp. 641–71, 1954.

years before President Roosevelt came to office and made it a part of his New Deal program. Other New Deal measures were advocated in Congress by members for several years before President Roosevelt put them on his "must" list. It should be noted that many important bills are enacted without the President's support, and, at times, despite his opposition.

TO HAVE OR NOT TO HAVE A BILL? "The legislative process is only one of the methods through which the contestants in the social struggle pursue their objectives," writes a perceptive student of the legislative process.[2] The same objective may often be achieved either through administrative action or legislation or possibly through judicial action, though usually with somewhat different results. The organization or group desiring a course of action must weigh the cost, time required, likelihood of success, and probable effects of each method. Some results can be achieved only by legislation. All department programs and activities must be authorized by law; no appropriation can be made until an activity is authorized. Before a new program may be instituted, an act must be passed authorizing the activity, usually specifying the objectives and defining the operations to be carried on, and perhaps limiting the amount of funds that may be expended.

Departments sometimes seek new authorizing legislation although they could initiate action under the authority of existing laws. Specific authorization of a new program arms the administrator with a congressional mandate that helps him to secure funds. President Eisenhower had ample constitutional authority to send armed forces to the Middle East and to the waters around Formosa, but he sought and secured advance congressional approval to strengthen his hand. Bills not requested by departments are sometimes introduced to spur executive officers to exercise authority that they already have or to exercise it more vigorously. The threat of such a law may produce the desired results without its passage.

Government departments hesitate to seek legislation unless there is a real need, and often get along with statutory provisions and restrictions that hamper their work, fearing that if they propose legislation

---

[2] Bertram Gross, *The Legislative Struggle,* McGraw-Hill Book Company, New York, 1953, p. 153.

Congress may write in provisions that they do not want. The difficulties of securing the passage of a bill are so great that standing committees are usually unwilling to bother with corrective legislation unless the need is urgent.

Bills are often introduced as a publicity device, as a rallying point for advocates of new government programs. Congress considers only specific legislative proposals; in order to secure consideration of a new policy or program, it must be put in the form of a bill. If proponents can persuade a committee to hold public hearings, they may secure nationwide publicity that would not be available in any other way. Bills are often introduced without any expectation that they will be passed, but to gain public support for a policy or program that may eventually lead to legislation.

THE LEGISLATIVE STRUGGLE

The administration bills proposed by the President and those requested by the executive departments have a much better chance of passage than bills without such support. They are virtually assured of being considered, while bills sponsored by private organizations and introduced by individual members must have strong backing to be considered. The President's bills are submitted to Congress with a special message that explains and defends his policy recommendations and states forcefully the need for the legislation. His message is reported in the daily press throughout the country, and is reproduced in full in *The New York Times* and in some other leading dailies. It is followed by editorial comments, usually favorable at this stage, and enterprising reporters interview leading members of both houses to publicize their views on the President's proposals.

To secure the adoption of his legislative program the President personally confers with the leaders of his party in both houses, the chairmen and ranking members of the committees, and other members of Congress whose support is needed. He is aided by a small liaison staff of persons who are widely and favorably known "on the Hill," whose function is to keep the President informed about congressional opinion and to aid congressional leaders in lining up the necessary support. The President, however, looks to the department primarily concerned with each bill to explain and defend it before Congress.

Department bills that are not included in the President's legislative program have many of the same advantages as administration bills. Every department has many strong supporters and friends among members of Congress, who usually support its legislative requests. In addition, departments are often able to enlist the active support of powerful interest groups, which are usually consulted in the preparation of bills. Department bills, however, must run the legislative gauntlet and, if they are controversial, will face strong opposition within Congress and by outside interest groups.

Bills sponsored by individual members, usually at the behest of outside groups and organizations, commonly face a much more difficult course. Without the publicity available to the President and to the executive departments, such bills have great difficulty in attracting national attention. Members pushing such legislation often try to secure the support, or at least acquiescence, of the administration. Bills that have the active support of leading members of Congress and powerful private organizations, however, are as likely to be passed as administration bills, especially if they have no strong opposition.

THE ROLE OF PRESSURE GROUPS A leading part in the legislative struggle is played by private organizations of all kinds, which are usually called "pressure groups" or "interest groups."[3] Because of the ability of such organizations to influence the course of legislation, especially to block legislation to which they are opposed, the terms "pressure groups" and "interest groups" are often used in a derogatory sense. The power that they wield, especially when several pressure groups work together, constitutes one of the major problems of democratic government. As a rule, they represent producers, while the great body of consumers is unorganized. A small body of men who have definite and specific interests of great concern to them, and who know exactly what they want and how to go about getting it, is more powerful than a large body of unorganized persons with less direct interest.

[3] See David Truman, *The Governmental Process*, Alfred A. Knopf, Inc., New York, 1953; Donald Blaisdell, *American Democracy Under Pressure*, The Ronald Press Company, New York, 1957; Gross, *The Legislative Struggle*, especially chaps. 2 and 3.

Yet the existence of private associations is inevitable in modern society. They are one of the principal means by which legislative bodies are informed of the wishes and desires of the great mass of citizens. They perform a useful, even indispensable, function of supplying legislators with information about policies and legislation under consideration. Their representatives, who like to be called "legislative counsel" or "legislative advocates" instead of lobbyists, are usually persons of ability and integrity. Legislators are able in most cases to rely upon the information supplied to them by the representatives of the leading interest groups.

Members of the "third house," as they are often called, are better paid, as a rule, than legislators. Many of them are former members of the legislative body. They have expert staffs which are usually better informed than congressional staffs. Pressure groups follow all legislation affecting their members, and occasionally sponsor bills, though their role is primarily defensive. They keep their members informed about all relevant legislation so that organized opposition or support may be delivered when needed. The more influential pressure groups have highly effective intelligence systems and inform their members about bills that are of concern to them, how much support each bill has, whether it is likely to pass, how it may best be defeated or amended, which members favor it, which are opposed, and which are undecided. Consequently, their campaigns are skillfully directed to gain the votes of particular members who can be influenced.

The legislative representatives of pressure groups appear before committees and present well-organized and informed arguments for or against pending bills, usually couched in terms of the national interest rather than their special interests. Their most effective work, however, is behind the scenes in private conversations with friendly legislators. In important legislative struggles, the heat is also turned on key members of Congress by local organizations and prominent citizens back home. A telephone call from a leading banker in the congressman's own district or from a prominent local industrialist or labor leader carries great weight, especially from persons who have made substantial contributions to the campaign fund of the congressman.

Private organizations also use other devices to influence legislative action. Large-scale publicity campaigns may be conducted to influence public opinion, as, for example, the campaigns conducted by the American Medical Association against health insurance and the Medicare program for the aged, or that of organized labor against the Taft-Hartley Act. Catchy slogans and epithets are often used in these campaigns. Thus, a bill to outlaw labor-management agreements for the closed shop is called "the right to work" bill; health insurance is denounced as "socialized medicine," and the Taft-Hartley Act is referred to as the "Slave-labor Act."

Pressure organizations are most effective in a propagandizing among their own members, and their lobbying activities are most effective with their own friends in Congress. Members of Congress are not neutral judges who weigh the evidence and pass upon legislative contests in a judicial manner. "What are the different classes of legislators," asked James Madison in *The Federalist* (No. 10), "but advocates and parties to the causes which they determine?" A leading authority on Congress has written:

> Today many of our legislators are little more than lobbyists in disguise for organized interests back home: cotton, tobacco, steel and textiles, cattle and wool and the like. They do not wait for pressure from their districts, but are prepared with speeches and briefs, amendments and arguments, to protect local and sectional interests.[4]

CONTROL OF LOBBYING Title III of the Legislative Reorganization Act of 1946 requires organizations and individuals whose *principal* activity is to influence legislation to register with the clerk of the House of Representatives and the clerk of the Senate, and to file financial statements of receipts and expenditures, including the purposes for which money was expended and the legislation they are paid to support or oppose. The limitation that only persons whose *principal* activity is lobbying are required to register provides a large loophole, permitting many to escape complying with the law. The act does not regulate lobbying as such, but merely seeks to require public disclosure of lobbying activities. It has been subject to much litigation.

In 1953, the Supreme Court held that the term "lobbying activities" meant direct representation before Congress, and not indirect

[4] George B. Galloway, *The Legislative Process in Congress,* Thomas Y. Crowell Company, New York, 1953, p. 514.

attempts to exert influence on legislation through a publicity campaign (*United States v. Rumeley,* 345 U.S. 41). This decision provides a second large loophole, for much lobbying activity is carried on through publicity campaigns. In 1966, the Joint Committee on the Organization of Congress recommended that the lobbying act be revised to require all organizations and persons conducting activities whose *substantial* purpose is to influence legislation to register and file financial reports. In an attempt to secure better enforcement of the act, the committee recommended that it be administered by the General Accounting Office, which would report any noncompliance to the Justice Department for appropriate action and submit annual reports to Congress. Earlier recommendations to strengthen the lobbying act were made by congressional committees in 1950 and 1951, but Congress failed to act. The 1970 Legislative Reorganization Act made no change in earlier law regulating lobbying, which is under investigation by another congressional committee. Congress appears to be in no hurry to enact additional regulation of lobbyists, aware that previous legislation has had little effect.

COMMITTEE HEARINGS AND MEETINGS

Most hearings conducted by congressional committees or subcommittees are to receive testimony with regard to pending bills that have been referred to them, but hearings are also used in investigations and inquiries into problem areas when no bill is under consideration. In addition, Senate committees conduct hearings on the President's nominations for major offices. Hearings may be open to the public or may be conducted in executive (closed) sessions, at the discretion of the committee or subcommittee. A majority of the members of the committee may order closed hearings when confidential testimony is to be taken, as, for example, testimony regarding national defense or foreign relations or when the members of the committee believe that an open hearing would not be in the public interest. The House Appropriations Committee as a matter of policy has long conducted most of its hearings on the federal budget in closed hearings, believing that departmental witnesses are willing to discuss their budget requests and plans more frankly in closed hearings. The hearings are subsequently published, but the departments are permitted to review the transcripts of their testimony and delete confidential materials and make minor editorial revisions before publication. The use of closed hearings when no confidential testimony is taken has frequently been criticized on the grounds that the public has a right to know and that public business should be transacted publicly.

In addition to hearings, committees hold meetings to discuss pending legislation and decide upon their recommendations, to "mark up" the bill, and to transact other business. Hearings are usually open to the public, but business meetings are usually conducted in executive (closed) sessions, which permits informal and frank discussion by committee members of their different points of view and facilitates agreements and compromises, which are an essential part of the legislative process.

The first step in considering a bill that has been referred to a committee is to decide whether to take it up, a decision that is ordinarily made by the chairman of the full committee. If the decision is favorable, he schedules a hearing or refers the bill to a subcommittee, which starts its consideration by scheduling hearings. Unless the chairman of the full committee is favorable, however, it is unlikely that he can be persuaded to schedule hearings. Individual members of Congress, as well as organized groups, often have serious difficulty in arousing sufficient interest in their bills to secure a public hearing. Usually they attempt to enlist the support of the executive department or agency concerned with the problem, but agency officials, "having been burned at the congressional stake too often, are wary."[5] The majority of bills considered by Congress today are administration bills, but there is no assurance that even these will be taken up by the committees to which they are referred. Ordinarily, the chairman of the committee to which the administration bill is referred, who has been consulted during the preparation of the bill, introduces it, especially if it is one of major importance. The chairman receives the honor of sponsoring the bill, which carries his name, and the executive department is assured of a hearing and the support of the chairman.

[5] See Clem Miller, *Member of the House,* Charles Scribner's Sons, New York, 1962, pp. 10–12.

Committee hearings on bills serve the following purposes: (1) They provide the essential information on the need for the legislation, the detailed provisions of the bill, and the probable results. (2) They provide a public forum in which proponents and opponents are heard. There is a strong feeling today that "due process" in considering proposed bills requires that all interested groups be given a reasonable opportunity to present their views, particularly on how the bill would affect them should it become law. (3) Hearings indicate which groups support the bill and which are opposed, and enable committee members to judge the size and strength of the contending forces and how strongly they feel about the proposed legislation. The testimony often indicates what revisions or compromises must be made in order to make the bill acceptable to a majority of the legislators. (4) The hearings may be used to publicize the proposed legislation and to arouse public support or mobilize opposition. The Senate committee hearings on automobile safety in 1966, for example, which were widely reported in the press and by radio and television, led to the enactment of legislation that before the hearings had little support in Congress.

During the hearings, the chairman and proponents of the bill under consideration attempt to build a record that will justify favorable action by the full committee and the House or Senate, while opponents attempt to build a record in opposition. The voluminous printed hearings, which may run several thousand pages in length, provide a source book for the use of both sides during the debate on the bill.

Most committee hearings rooms are imposing and conducive to formal proceedings. The committee members are seated in a semicircle on an elevated dais, the chairman in the center, with the majority-party members seated in order of rank on one side and the minority-party members on the other. Immediately in front of the chairman and seated at a lower level are members of the committee staff and the official reporter; witnesses and the public are seated beyond a railing. A public address system is used. Important Senate hearings are often televised, but before 1971 House committee hearings were not because of the opposition of the Speaker and party leaders. The Legislative Reorganization Act of 1970 authorizes the televising and broadcasting over radio of House committee hearings. Subcommittee hearings are often conducted in smaller rooms, often with the members and witnesses seated at the table and the public seated around the room. Their proceedings are usually conducted in a somewhat less formal manner than those of the full committees.

If the proposed bill is a part of the President's legislative program or is sponsored by an executive department, which is true of most important bills today, the head of the department concerned will usually be the first witness called when the hearings are opened. His appearance is expected by the members of the committee as a courtesy and usually receives national publicity. The department head ordinarily makes a general statement about the purposes of the legislation, leaving the details to be discussed by subordinates who follow him. Department witnesses may occupy several days, or even longer if the bill is one of major importance, and are usually called back later in the hearings to supply additional information. Although the department head is treated with deference by members of the committee, other department witnesses may be subjected to a grilling by members who are opposed to the legislation.

The decision as to who will be invited to testify rests largely with the chairman. The leading interest groups supporting or opposed to the legislation customarily request permission to testify, which with few exceptions is granted. Included among the witnesses are usually experts, real or supposed, spokesmen for the various interest groups, representatives of organized labor, and a sprinkling of university professors. Both sides endeavor to produce prominent witnesses whose testimony will carry weight with members of the committee and be reported in the press. Opponents may seek to delay action by producing a large number of persons to testify in an attempt to arouse opposition to the bill.

Witnesses are legally required to submit a written statement of their testimony in advance, but this requirement is not always observed, and many witnesses submit such a statement when they appear before the committee. Usually the witness is asked to summarize the main points of his statement, copies of which are placed in the hands of all members of the committee, but if the witness is an important personage and his statement is brief, he is permitted to read it. Few witnesses are permitted to proceed more than a few minutes, however, before they are interrupted by questions of members of the committee, often prefaced by lengthy statements that take more time than the testimony of the witness.

It might be assumed that committee members act as impartial judges, seeking to bring out the facts and to elicit the opinions of witnesses, but this is seldom the case. Most members of committees usually have already made up their minds about proposed legislation before the hearings start, and they do not hesitate to express their own opinions during the hearings. They are active participants in the legislative struggle between contending forces in the hearings and seek to build a record that will support their own positions. Often they preface questions by a lengthy statement of their own views and seek to elicit answers that corroborate their opinions. Friendly witnesses are treated deferentially, asked leading questions, and praised for their statements, while opposing witnesses may be badgered by members who wish to discredit their testimony. Such discourtesies to witnesses by a few committee members are often embarrassing to other members and lessen the prestige of Congress, but are accepted as a part of the rough-and-tumble of the political struggle.

After the hearings are concluded, the chairman of the committee or subcommittee usually holds a meeting or caucus with the majority-party committee members in an attempt to reach an agreement on what action will be taken and to secure party unity when the committee meets in executive session to act on the pending bill. At this point, concessions will usually be made where necessary to secure the support of wavering members. The minority-party members similarly meet to decide upon position and strategy.

When the committee meets in executive session to "mark up" a bill, only committee members and the committee staff are in attendance, though occasionally a department official may be invited to attend in order to provide technical information but not to participate otherwise. The bill is read section by section and amendments may be offered, usually by those who are opposed to the bill. The chairman usually strongly opposes such amendments, attempting to hold the line on the bill as agreed to in party caucus, knowing that if opponents are able to divide the majority and amend the bill, it may be amended to death. Often party lines do not hold, and those in favor of the bill must fight to prevent its emasculation by amendments at this stage.

Committee members who expect to be absent usually leave their proxies with the chairman or the ranking minority-party member, and proxy votes often decide the action of the committee. The use of proxy voting in committee has been criticized because the absent member does not always know on what issues his proxy may be used; and, if he had been present at the discussion which precedes the vote, he might have voted differently. The Joint Committee on the Organization of Congress in 1966 recommended that proxy voting in committee be prohibited, but the 1970 Reorganization Act makes use of it discretionary with each committee.

What transpires in executive sessions of committees is regarded as secret but is often leaked to the press in garbled form. Votes cast by members in committee have heretofore been regarded as confidential. The 1970 Legislative Reorganization Act provides that roll-call votes in Senate committees, including how each member voted, shall be publicly announced by the committees, and that House committees shall keep a record of roll-call votes, which shall be open for public inspection. It should be noted, however, that the requirement applies only to committees and does not apply to subcommittees. Also, it applies only to *roll-call* votes and may be avoided by not calling the roll. In the past, the secrecy of committee votes has permitted members to vote in committee contrary to their publicly announced positions, knowing that their constituents will be unaware of their vote in committee. The required publication of how each member voted on roll-call votes in committee will, to some extent, make members more responsible to their constituents.

Bills that have been approved by a subcommittee are reported to the full committee and require its approval before being reported to the House or Senate. Subcommittees, which are usually jealous of their prerogatives, fight hard in defense of their bills and oppose amendments by the full committee. Usually the full committee approves the bill as recommended; but at times a fight occurs in the full committee over provisions of the bill, and it may be amended or defeated.

When a bill is reported to the House or Senate it is accompanied by a printed report summarizing its provisions and presenting the principal arguments for its passage. Committee members who oppose the bill may submit a minority report. The majority report is prepared by the staff under the direction of the chairman, but it must be approved by the full committee before it is submitted to the parent house. A draft report is usually prepared by the subcommittee and is submitted to the full committee along with the bill.

PROCEDURE IN THE HOUSE

The rules of procedure of the House, which have developed over the years, are highly detailed. Not only has the House adopted and revised from time to time its rules, which are set forth in the House Manual, but the rulings of the Speakers and the chairmen of the committee of the whole constitute precedents that govern its deliberations. These rulings have been published in an 11-volume work, *Hind's and Cannon's Precedents of the House of Representatives.* Only a few of the more important procedures will be discussed here.

Bills are introduced merely by sending them to the clerk's desk. The House does not permit joint sponsorship of bills, as is the practice in the Senate, and hence identical bills are often introduced by a number of members. House bills bear the letters "H.R."; Senate bills are designated by the letter "S." followed by a number. After introduction, bills are referred by the Speaker to the proper committee, usually on advice of the Parliamentarian. If a bill is approved by the standing committee to which it is referred, usually after numerous revisions, it is reported back to the House and is placed on one of the several calendars of bills. Finance bills are placed on the *Union Calendar* and, being privileged, may be called up for consideration by the chairman of the committee when he is recognized (by prearrangement) by the Speaker. Other public bills are placed on the *House Calendar;* private bills are placed on the *Private Calendar;* and noncontroversial bills may be transferred to the *Consent Calendar.* Bills on the House Calendar are not taken up in order, but only when a special rule is brought in by the Rules Committee. Bills on the Union Calendar may be taken up without benefit of a special rule, but in practice the finance committees usually ask for a rule in order to limit debate and amendments that may be made from the floor. Bills on the Private Calendar and Consent Calendar are taken up on designated days.

THE HOUSE RULES COMMITTEE The major functions of the Rules Committee are to determine which bills reported by the standing committee will be taken up by the House and to recommend special rules for the consideration of each bill. The special rule prescribes the length of general debate on the bill and whether it will be considered under an "open" rule, which places no restriction on the amendments that may be offered from the floor, or a "closed" rule, which limits amendments and in some cases does not permit any amendment to be offered from the floor. The chairmen of standing committees, after reporting a bill to the House, apply to the Rules Committee for a special rule, which, if adopted by a majority vote of the House, makes the bill in order for immediate consideration by the House.

There are usually more bills reported by standing legislative committees than there is time for the House to consider, and some means is needed to select those of greater importance and bring them before the House for its consideration, and to pass over bills of lesser importance and those that are likely to be rejected by the House. In addition, there is need for a screening committee that will reject bills that are contrary to the public interest but that if brought to a vote will likely be passed because of the pressures upon members of Congress. The standing committees cannot always be relied upon to reject such bills, for they consist largely of members who are in favor of the programs that they pass upon. For example, if there were no screening committee, the Committee on Veterans' Affairs would probably report bills providing unwarranted increases in veterans' pensions and other benefits, bills that a majority of members would feel compelled to vote for, irrespective of their merits.

In the early history of Congress, the sole function of the Rules Committee was to consider proposed changes in the standing rules, but after 1880 it became the agenda committee, determining which committee bills would be acted upon by the House. It became the instrument of the Speaker, who was the leader of the majority party, to assure that administration bills would be given priority. The revolt against the Speaker in 1910 stripped him of most of his powers, including the chairmanship of the Rules Committee but did not remove the power of the Rules Committee to determine which bills would be considered. On the contrary, as the Speaker's powers declined, those of the Rules Committee increased. From 1910 until 1937, the committee continued to act as the instrument of the majority-party leadership to assure consideration of legislation that it sponsored. In order to assure a working majority of the committee, the majority party always insisted upon having twice as many members as the minority party.

But by 1937, a bipartisan coalition of dissident Democrats and conservative Republicans who were united in their opposition to President Roosevelt's legislative program had come to dominate the committee, and the House Democratic leadership was forced to use the discharge petition to get the bill that became the Wages and Hours Act of 1938 to the floor.[6]

Since 1937, when the Democrats have been in control of the House, a coalition of Southern conservative Democrats and Northern conservative Republicans have usually controlled the Rules Committee and have often blocked bills supported by the Democratic party leadership on civil rights, wages and hours, labor-management relations, education, welfare, and some other subjects. Instead of functioning as an instrument of the majority-party leadership, it has often blocked major bills of the party. The committee has come to consider its function not as that of a traffic controller of legislation to see that adequate time is provided to consider the most important legislation, particularly bills sponsored by the majority-party leadership, but rather that of supervising and passing upon the policies of legislation reported by the standing committees. This assumption of power was strongly condemned by Rep. Herman P. Eberharter (D) of Pennsylvania in a letter to his colleagues in 1948, as follows:

In theory the Rules Committee is a traffic director on the legislative highway, determining the order of business on the floor of the House. In practice this committee has become an obstruction to orderly traffic. The committee often allows bills to come before the House only on its own terms. It frequently usurps the functions of the regular legislative commit-

[6]Milton C. Cummings, Jr., and Robert L. Peabody, "The Decision to Enlarge the Committee on Rules: An Analysis of the 1961 Vote" in Robert L. Peabody and Nelson W. Polsby (eds.), *New Perspectives on the House of Representatives,* Rand McNally & Company, Chicago, 1963, p. 170.

tees of the House by holding hearings and reviewing the merits of bills that have already been carefully studied by the proper legislative committees. A reform of this undemocratic system is long overdue.[7]

Testifying before the Joint Committee on the Organization of Congress in 1965, Rep. Chet Holifield of California criticized the Rules Committee for placing "roadblocks in the way of many important legislative measures."

There is no need to have the Committee on Rules impose its own judgment on policy matters which legislative committees have decided and which should be passed upon by the House itself. . . . The Rules Committee is not an expert in the field of atomic energy. They are not expert in the field of space. They are not an expert in the field of agriculture. . . . They do not have the jurisdictional expertise in all of this subject matter which the members of the committee study for years. I say that when a majority of a committee decides that a bill is in the national interest, whether it be good or bad, that it should be allowed to have its test upon the floor and let the full membership of the House decide whether it is good or bad, not the majority of any small committee. This is a matter of principle that I believe in. . . . The Committee on Rules should not substitute its own judgment for that of the standing committees, nor prevent the House from working its will.[8]

When the Rules Committee reports a special rule to the House to permit a bill to be made the order of business, it determines the shape of the bill to be voted on by the House. If the committee favors a bill, it may expedite its passage by limiting the time for debate and restricting the amendments that may be offered from the floor. It may even prohibit any amendments from being offered from the floor. If a majority of members of the committee are opposed to a bill, they may refuse to grant a rule, which is required for it to be considered by the House; or they may report the bill without any limit on the time for debate or upon amendments that may be offered from the floor, thus

[7] Quoted in George B. Galloway, *History of the House of Representatives,* Thomas Y. Crowell Company, New York, 1961, p. 61.

[8] *Hearings,* 89th Cong., 1st Sess., part 2, p. 193.

permitting opponents to "talk the bill to death" or to emasculate it with crippling amendments.

REVOLT AGAINST THE RULES COMMITTEE Since 1949, there has been continual criticism of the Rules Committee for blocking consideration of important legislative measures, and various proposals have been advanced to curb its powers. Liberals have urged reduction of its powers, but the large majority of Republicans and a sizable minority of conservative Democrats have opposed any change. In 1949, when the Democrats regained control of the House, the rules were amended to provide that after a bill had been held for 21 days by the Rules Committee the Speaker could recognize a member of the standing committee that reported the bill to make a motion to take it up; and, if the motion was passed by a majority, the bill would be made the order of business, thus bypassing the Rules Committee. The rule proved effective; eight important bills for which the Rules Committee had refused a rule were taken up under the 21-days rule and passed. A number of other bills that the Rules Committee would ordinarily have refused were granted a rule. Two years later, however, the liberal Democrats lost a number of seats in the House and the House repealed the 21-days rule.

In 1960, the issue of the power of the Rules Committee to block legislation arose in the midst of a presidential campaign when it refused to permit three bills providing federal aid to education, public housing, and minimum wages, which had been passed by both houses in slightly different form, to be sent to conference committees to reconcile the differences, which killed all three bills for the session. The Democratic platform specifically pledged to enact such legislation; John F. Kennedy, the Democratic candidate for President, and the party leadership in the House attempted in vain to persuade the committee to permit the bills to be sent to conference, but the six conservative members of the committee refused and Congress adjourned without acting on the bills.

When Congress met in 1961, it was apparent that unless the power of the conservative coalition of the Rules Committee to block legislation was curbed, it would be impossible to bring President Kennedy's legislative program before the House for its consideration and action. Democratic Speaker Rayburn agreed to accept responsibility for securing a revision of the rules or other changes that would enable the Presidential legislative program to be brought before the House. After considering various proposals, he decided upon increase of the size of the committee from 12 to 15 members, thus affording an opportunity to add two liberal Democrats to the committee to offset the votes of Chairman Howard W. Smith and Rep. William M. Colmer. The addition of two liberal Democrats and one conservative Republican gave the liberal Democrats a razor-thin margin of one vote. The plan did not unseat any present member of the committee, which had been proposed, and was the minimum change that would assure that the administration bills would not be blocked by the committee.

The Democrats endorsed the plan in caucus by a divided vote, and the Republican caucus opposed it. The fight over the plan was intense and was widely reported in the press. John D. Morris of *The New York Times* wrote that the power and prestige of "two tough and skillful septuagenarians"—Rayburn and Smith—rode on the outcome.[9] Chairman Smith and the Republican leaders charged that the proposal was an attempt to "pack or purge" the Committee on Rules. In the debate, Chairman Smith promised to cooperate with the Democratic leadership "just as long and as far as my conscience will permit me to go," but ironically declared that on "any resolution or bill in this House that I am conscientiously opposed to, I would not yield my conscience and my right to vote in this House to any person or any member or under any conditions."[10] Thus stoutly defending his right to vote on any bill or resolution "in this House," Smith appeared oblivious of the fact that the Rules Committee often deprives other members of the right to vote on important legislation.

In closing the debate, Speaker Rayburn took the floor to urge the adoption of his proposal to enlarge the Rules Committee in order to assure that bills reported by committees to carry out the President's legislative program would not be blocked by the committee. "I think this House," he said, "should be allowed on the great measures to work its will, and it cannot work its will if the Committee on Rules is so constituted as not to allow the House to pass on those things. . . . Let

[9] Quoted in Cummings and Peabody, "The Decision to Enlarge the Committee . . . ," p. 177.
[10] *Ibid.*, p. 178.

us move this program."[11] The proposal to enlarge the committee passed by a vote of 217 to 212. It was saved by 22 liberal Republicans who voted with 195 Democrats for the enlargement, while 64 Democrats and 148 Republicans voted against. Loyalty to Rayburn was probably largely responsible for the votes of 36 Southern Democrats for the proposal, while 62 Southern Democrats voted against it.

When the Rules Committee met, Chairman Smith announced that the three new members were temporary additions to the committee and arranged that ordinary chairs would be provided for them at the foot of the table instead of the large leather upholstered chairs reserved for members. The effect of the enlargement of the committee was not as great as those who voted for the change had hoped, or as those opposing had feared. The committee functioned very much the same as it had in the preceding Congress; it refused to grant a rule for 11 bills, the same number refused in the preceding Congress; it continued to use its power to require changes in committee bills before granting a rule; and it continued to report about the same number of closed rules (22), which prohibited amendments from being proposed from the floor. All of the administration bills except two—federal aid to education and the creation of a new department of urban affairs—were granted rules; nevertheless, President Kennedy failed to secure the enactment of most of his bills in the Eighty-seventh Congress (1961–1963). Two years later, the enlargement of the committee was made permanent by a large majority.[12]

Following the Democratic landslide victory in 1964, in which more than 40 new Democratic liberals were elected from the North and the West, the House adopted two significant changes in its rules that increased the powers of the Speaker and reduced those of the Rules Committee. One change was to permit the Speaker to entertain a motion from the floor to send a bill passed by both houses to conference without the necessity of having a rule from the Rules Committee. The other change was to reinstate the 21-days rule to permit the Speaker to bypass the Rules Committee after it had held a bill for 21

[11] *Ibid.*

[12] See James A. Robinson, *The House Rules Committee,* The Bobbs-Merrill Company, Inc., Indianapolis, 1963, pp. 78–80.

days. This rule was invoked six times in 1965 and none of President Johnson's bills was blocked by the committee. Speaker Carl Albert urged the adoption of the 21-days rule in 1971, but it was defeated by the House.

In 1966, Rep. Howard W. Smith, one of the most conservative members of the House and for many years chairman of the Rules Committee, was defeated for reelection at the age of 83. At times, Smith refused to call a meeting of the Rules Committee to consider a bill that he opposed. In 1957, when a rule was requested near the end of the session for a civil rights bill that he opposed, he left the city, leaving word that he had gone to his farm in nearby Virginia to inspect a barn that had been burned. Speaker Rayburn was reported to have exclaimed on hearing about Smith's absence: "I knew Howard Smith would do almost anything to block a civil rights bill, but I never suspected he would resort to arson."[13] Representative William M. Colmer of Pascagoula, Mississippi, a strong conservative who invariably had voted with Smith, succeeded him as chairman. He has served in Congress since 1933 and was 81 years of age in 1971.

COMMITTEE OF THE WHOLE In considering most bills, the House resolves itself into the committee of the whole. When the House is in regular session, the Speaker presides and a majority of all members (218) must be present to constitute a quorum for the transaction of business. When the House resolves itself into the committee of the whole, the Speaker withdraws and another member he has designated presides. Only 100 members are required to constitute a quorum in the committee of the whole, and the procedure is more informal than when the House is in regular session. The rules allow members only five minutes to speak on proposed amendments. The debate is pertinent and pointed, and consideration of bills moves rapidly without long-winded speeches. No roll-call vote is taken, which saves much time, and quorum calls are seldom used as a dilatory tactic, since only 100 members constitute a quorum. When the committee of the whole has completed its work for the day, it resolves itself into regular session and the Speaker returns to the chair.

[13] *Ibid.,* p. 209.

VOTING IN THE HOUSE Votes in the House are taken in five ways: (1) by voice vote, in which the presiding officer determines whether the ayes or nays are in a majority; (2) by division, in which members stand and are counted by the presiding officer; (3) by teller count, in which members file through the aisle and are counted by tellers; (4) by "tellers with clerk," in which a record of how each member voted is made; and (5) by roll call. Before 1971, no record was made of how each member voted in the committee of the whole, or whether they voted at all, which permitted members to be absent without incurring the danger of missing a roll-call vote. If a member was opposed to a

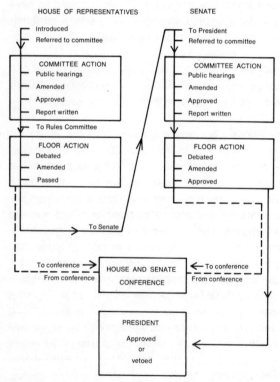

The steps by which a bill becomes a law. Bills may be introduced in either house.

bill that was popular in his district, he could vote in the committee of the whole for an emasculating amendment that in effect killed the bill, and later vote for the bill on the roll-call vote on passage of the bill. Thus he could claim that he voted for the bill without disclosing that on the key vote in the committee of the whole he had voted for an amendment to emasculate it. The rules were amended in 1970 by the Legislative Reorganization Act to provide for a "tellers with clerks" count, which may be used in the committee of the whole if requested by one-fifth of the quorum of 100 members. This change in the rules will remove the secrecy of how members vote on key amendments in the committee of the whole and make them more responsible to their constituents.

When the House is in regular session, a roll-call vote may be required by one-fifth of those present. When the roll is called, electric bells ring in the House office buildings to enable members who are in their offices to come to the chamber in time to be recorded. Roll-call votes, each of which requires about three-quarters of an hour, take up a vast amount of time of the House during each session. Many state legislatures have installed electric voting which permits a roll-call vote to be taken and recorded in less than a minute, but the House has been unwilling to install electric voting, which would make it necessary for members to be in constant attendance when the House is in session lest they miss roll-call votes. Much of the debate in the House is desultory and of little or no interest to the great majority of members, who prefer to spend their time in their offices attending to legislative business rather than wasting it by being in constant attendance.

The time allotted for debate in the House is strictly controlled. For more than 100 years the House has limited the time during which any member may speak to one hour, but speeches of this length are practically unknown because of the limited time allowed for debate of even the most important measures. The rule under which a bill is brought up limits the time allowed for debate, one-half being allotted to members favoring the bill and one-half to opponents. Customarily the chairman of the committee reporting the bill, or another member designated by him, has charge of the time allocated for proponents, and the time of opponents is controlled by the ranking minority member of the committee. Most of the allotted time is taken by members of the committee reporting the bill, and the remaining time is divided among others who wish to speak. Often members who are granted limited time ask permission to extend their remarks in the record.

The quality of the debate in the House leaves much to be desired. Visitors to the galleries are often shocked at the small attendance when routine business is being conducted, but many members of Congress find it necessary to be absent at such times in order to take care of more important work on committees and to handle the requests of constituents. At times the debate is lively, pertinent, and well attended, especially when the debate on important bills nears a close and the party leaders on each side make the closing statements. The debate on amendments in the committee of the whole, during which speakers are limited to five minutes, moves at a rapid pace and those who speak are usually well informed, but at other times the debate is not impressive. Many speeches on the floor are designed for home consumption. Few votes are changed by the debates; when in doubt most members rely largely upon the judgment of the committee members of their party rather than upon speeches on the floor.

Debate is virtually a lost art in the House, due in large part to the severe time limitations placed on it. When only a few hours are allowed to debate an important and complex measure, and the allotted 'time is divided among many members who want to express their views, no member has sufficient time to discuss the various provisions of the bill with any degree of thoroughness. Aware of these limitations, as well as of the fact that debates seldom influence votes, members are not encouraged to prepare for them, and the debates often degenerate into platitudes and clichés, with frequent pleas for support of the President, the party, or the leadership.

PROCEDURE IN THE SENATE

The Senate, a much smaller body than the House of Representatives, is able to transact its business more informally and without strict rules of procedure. Much of its business is transacted under suspension of the rules by unanimous consent. The Senate does not operate under special rules, as the House does. The Senate committee on Rules does not act as a screening body to select the bills that will be brought before the Senate for its consideration. The Senate itself decides which bills it will take up. By custom, motions to take up particular bills are made by the majority leader, but may be made by others. The majority leader does not have the power to decide which bills will be considered, but he has a great deal of influence in determining the order in which bills are considered.

The Senate acts on measures without the use of a committee of the whole. It does not use several calendars as does the House but all reported bills are placed on the Calendar of the Senate, from which they may be taken for consideration by a majority vote. Custom and tradition have greater influence than formal rules, though the Senate has a large body of rules that were first compiled by Thomas Jefferson when he was Vice President.

THE FILIBUSTER One of the most notable features of Senate procedure is that the rules permit unlimited debate. With certain exceptions, a senator on being recognized may hold the floor as long as he desires and is able to remain standing. He does not have to confine his remarks to the subject before the chamber, but may speak on wholly irrelevant matters. The absence of the requirement of relevance often leads to a disconnected debate on important legislation. During the debate on a major bill a member may secure the floor and make a speech on the beauties of his home state or anything else that he wishes to talk about; the Senate quickly empties, except for two or three members who wearily wait until the debate can be resumed. This kind of irrelevant debate is frowned upon by the members of the "Inner Club."

The Senate prides itself on being the only major legislative chamber in the world that has no rules restricting the length of time members may speak. Yet time limits are in fact placed on debate, for only by adopting such restrictions can any legislative body transact its business. Much of the business of the Senate is transacted by unanimous consent and many important bills are passed with little or no debate, but controversial measures are usually debated at great length. Senate debates often affect the outcome by informing and arousing public opinion. After debate on a bill has proceeded for several days and the principal proponents and opponents have made lengthy speeches, the majority leader is usually able to secure a unanimous agreement fixing a time when debate will end and the Senate will proceed to vote on the bill and all amendments. By this time everything that can be said for and against the bill has probably been said, and further continuation of the debate would be tedious.

In the early history of the Senate the rules permitted the previous question to be moved, the usual device for closing debate, but this rule was dropped in 1806 and thereafter until 1917 there was no provision whereby a majority could bring debate to an end and force a vote to be taken. Before 1841, little use was made of the filibuster, that is, prolonged debate, to prevent a vote from being taken. After a prolonged filibuster in 1841, however, Henry Clay proposed the adoption of a one-hour rule, saying, "Let our contests be of intellectuality, and not of physical force in seeing who could sit out the other or consume the most time in useless debate."[14]

Before 1933, when the second or "short" session of Congress ended on March 4, the filibuster (which prevents other business from being transacted) was highly effective in the closing days of the session. Individual senators often resorted to the filibuster to secure appropriations for their states, holding the floor until the Senate leaders agreed to yield to their demands. Senator Ben Tillman of South Carolina conducted a filibuster in 1903 to force the Senate to include an item in the appropriation bill to pay a claim of his state. Securing the floor a few hours before the Senate was required to adjourn, he proceeded to read from Byron's *Childe Harold* until his colleagues agreed to the item. Similarly, Sen. William J. Stone of Missouri once conducted a filibuster to force an appropriation for a new post office building in St. Louis.

In 1908, the elder Sen. Robert M. La Follette of Wisconsin led a filibuster against the Vreeland-Aldrich Currency Bill, which lasted 28 days but finally failed.

In 1917, a filibuster of 11 senators blocked the passage of a bill urged by President Wilson to authorize the arming of merchant vessels. The United States was still neutral and the filibustering senators feared that the passage of the bill would lead the country into World War I. The House had passed the bill with only a few dissenting votes. President Wilson made a historic attack on the 11 filibustering sena-

---

[14] Quoted by Lindsay Rogers, *The American Senate,* F. S. Crofts & Co., New York, 1926, p. 166.

tors and the rules of the Senate which permitted a few members to block action in a crisis:

> The Senate of the United States is the only legislative body in the world which cannot act when a majority is ready for action. A little group of wilful men, representing no opinion but their own, have rendered the great government of the United States helpless and contemptible. . . . The only remedy is that the rules of the Senate shall be so altered that it can act.[15]

Four days later, the Senate adopted a cloture rule under which 16 senators may petition to limit debate and if a two-thirds majority vote in favor of cloture, members of the Senate are limited thereafter to one hour each. The cloture rule has continued in effect, though subsequently modified, but it has been successfully invoked only six times in 50 years. Numerous attempts have been made at other times to invoke cloture, but have failed to secure the required two-thirds majority.

A successful filibuster requires the concerted efforts of a group of senators who are able to prolong debate by lengthy speeches and dilatory tactics until the majority of the Senate agrees to table the measure under consideration, in order that essential legislation may be taken up. Filibustering senators usually make little pretense of speaking on the bill before the Senate; with their desks piled high with books and papers, they talk or read on any subject of their choosing. Fellow senators often help out by asking lengthy questions, which may take a half hour or even longer, thus providing the senator who has the floor with a "breather." Another delaying tactic is for a colleague to observe to the presiding officer that a quorum is not present; this requires a quorum call to bring in a majority of senators before the debate may be resumed. During filibusters the Senate is often held in continuous sessions in an attempt to wear out the filibustering senators and force them to yield the floor. The struggle becomes one of endurance until one side gives way.

In recent years, the filibuster has been used principally by Southern senators to block votes on civil rights legislation, including bills relating to the right to vote, segregation, lynching, and fair employment

[15] *The Washington Post,* March 15, 1917.

practices. Senators favoring civil rights legislation have tried unsuccessfully to amend the rules to permit a majority of senators present and voting to impose cloture. Regardless of the rules, it is difficult to invoke cloture, as the experience of the past 50 years indicates, for the majority of senators are reluctant to vote any limitation on debate.

"Our position has been misrepresented. We only want to deny the U.S. Senate the right to vote." (Herblock in *The Washington Post & Times Herald.*)

The right of unlimited debate has on occasion been used by senators to present the issues and extend the debate until the public became informed and until the force of public opinion could be brought to bear on the outcome. Thus, a small group of liberal senators carried on an extended debate in 1962 in opposition to the administration bill to set up a private corporation to develop and operate a space-satellite communication system. For the first time in 35 years, the Senate adopted a cloture rule to limit debate. On numerous occasions senators have thus been able to force the adoption of important amendments to pending bills. Senators who have spoken at great length against bills which they regard as contrary to public interest contend that a lengthy speech on the merits of a bill, which is intended to inform the country and to delay but not prevent a vote from being taken, is not a filibuster, for the purpose of a filibuster is to prevent a pending bill or motion from coming to a vote.

The filibuster enables a determined minority of senators to prevent legislation which they regard as obnoxious from coming to a vote. Its effect is to require not merely a majority of the Senate, but a concurrent majority of senators from all major sections of the country to approve proposed legislation. The Constitution protects the rights of minorities as well as of majorities. A group of senators large enough to carry on a successful filibuster and sufficiently determined to withstand the pressure of public opinion can prevent the government from taking an action that their section regards as unacceptable.

During the past 20 years repeated attempts have been made by a group of liberal senators (some of whom have used the filibuster to oppose legislation) to revise Rule 22 of the Senate by reducing the majority required to vote cloture from two-thirds to 60 percent. So far their efforts have been unsuccessful, but the number of senators voting in favor of revising the rule has steadily increased. The change is strongly opposed by practically all Southern senators and by senators from other parts of the country who are unwilling to see the right of unlimited debate curtailed.

The right of members to speak without limit is a highly prized tradition of the Senate and one that it is reluctant to give up. When wisely used by senators who are thoroughly prepared and speak on issues of national importance, their lengthy speeches serve to educate the country and to arouse public opinion; however, such speeches are frequently made by senators whose loquacity exceeds their sagacity. The senators who have the greatest influence on the course of legislation rarely speak at length. It is the function of legislative bodies not only to debate but also to act. Action without debate is unwise and dangerous; debate without action is futile and renders the government impotent in dealing with the pressing problems of society. One of the principal causes of the rise of dictatorships in other countries has been the public distrust and disgust with a legislative body that can only talk but cannot act when events demand action.

REVIEW QUESTIONS

1. What are the major sources of bills in Congress? Why is there a growing trend for important bills to be submitted by the President and the executive departments? What effect does this trend have on the authority of Congress?

2. What functions do pressure groups serve in the legislative process? How do pressure groups influence legislation and why are they powerful?

3. Describe federal regulation of lobbyists. Why is it ineffective?

4. What are the several purposes of committee hearings on proposed legislation?

5. Why were the rules changed in 1970 to require publication of roll-call votes in committee? Criticize the use of proxy votes in committee.

6. What are the functions and powers of the House Rules Committee? Give the arguments pro and con for reducing the power of the Rules Committee. What is the 21-days rule and what were its effects?

7. Why does the House use a committee of the whole in considering amendments to pending bills? Why doesn't the Senate use a committee of the whole?

8. Why is the quality of debate in the House generally criticized?

6 LEGISLATIVE-EXECUTIVE RELATIONS

THE PRESIDENT AS CHIEF LEGISLATOR

RECENT DEVELOPMENT The study of Congress would not be complete without an account of the role of the President in the legislative process—a role that has greatly increased during the present century. All Presidents have made recommendations to Congress for legislation in the State of the Union message at the opening of each session, but until this century they have not presented a legislative program and worked with the leaders to secure its sdoption. James G. Bryce stated in his famous work *The American Commonwealth,* published in 1888, that the President's messages do not have "any more effect on Con-

157

gress than an article in a prominent newspaper . . . and, in fact, the suggestions which he makes, year after year, are usually neglected, even when his party has a majority in both houses."[1]

President Theodore Roosevelt during the first decade of this century recommended many legislative measures to Congress, taking the position that "a good executive under present conditions of American life must take a very active interest in getting the right kind of legislation."[2] Woodrow Wilson, however, was the first President to take active leadership in securing the passage of his legislative program, and in his first term more important legislation was enacted than during the preceding half century. He worked closely with the Democratic party leadership in Congress and his chief legislative measures were approved in the party caucus, binding party members to support them. With eloquence the President enlisted public support for his legislative program; and his party, long out of office, followed his lead. Before he became President he had written his concept of the Presidency, which he later carried out in office.

> His is the only national voice in affairs. Let him once win the admiration and confidence of the country, and no other single force can withstand him, no combination of forces will easily overpower him. His position takes the imagination of the country. He is the representative of no constituency, but the whole people. When he speaks in his true character, he speaks for no special interest. If he rightly interpret the national thought and boldly insist upon it, he is irresistible; and the country never feels the zest of action so much as when its President is of such insight and calibre.[3]

After Wilson, the pendulum of public opinion swung away from strong presidents, and Warren G. Harding was elected on a pledge not to exercise legislative leadership and to return the country to "normalcy." He was followed by Calvin Coolidge, who believed that

---

[1] The Macmillan Company, New York, 1906 ed., vol. I, p. 230.

[2] Quoted in Clinton Rossiter, *The American Presidency,* Harcourt, Brace & World, Inc., New York, 1960, p. 77.

[3] Woodrow Wilson, *Constitutional Government in the United States,* Columbia University Press, New York, 1908, p. 68.

there were already too many laws on the statute books, recommended little legislation to Congress, and made little or no effort to secure its adoption. When President Franklin D. Roosevelt took office in 1933, the country was in the midst of the Great Depression. During the first Hundred Days of his administration Congress enacted his legislative bills to cope with the emergency without much discussion or opposition. A consummate politician, Roosevelt was able in his first term to secure the enactment of legislation greatly expanding the functions of the federal government to deal with the social and economic ills of society, but Congress increasingly chafed under his leadership and the accusation that it had become a "rubber stamp." After his reelection in 1936 by an unprecedented majority, he shortly proposed legislation to increase the size of the Supreme Court, which had held several New Deal measures unconstitutional. There ensued a bitter fight over the "court packing" plan, which was eventually defeated. Thereafter, Roosevelt faced increased difficulties in securing the enactment of his legislative program. After the United States entered World War II, domestic legislation was laid on the shelf. The President was able to secure approval of his war-related measures, but not without a fight.

The pattern of legislative leadership by the President was established by Roosevelt. In his messages on the State of the Union, he set forth eloquently the broad objectives of his legislative programs, which were followed by special messages proposing specific legislation. Bills drafted by the executive departments or commissions to carry out his recommendations were introduced by friendly members of Congress, often by the chairmen of the committees to which the bills would be referred. Protocol did not yet permit the President to submit a draft of a bill to carry out his recommendation. Roosevelt limited his recommendations to major bills that he thought could be enacted, but after his first term he faced increasing difficulties in getting his bills through Congress.

President Truman followed a different course of submitting numerous recommendations of legislation without regard to their chances of passage, and as a consequence relatively few of his bills were enacted. President Eisenhower came into office without a legislative program, but the requirements of the country forced him to submit modest programs. In the main, he was successful in securing the enactment of his legislative recommendations and the defeat of measures that he opposed, although in six of the eight years he was in office the Democrats controlled Congress. In foreign affairs, he had the support of the Democratic leaders. Eisenhower had the assistance of a legislative staff of several persons in his relations with the leaders and members of Congress. In the last years in office, he used the veto power effectively to block legislation to which he was opposed, with the solid support of Republican members.

Before taking office in 1961, President John F. Kennedy appointed a number of task forces composed of outstanding citizens and experts to prepare recommendations for legislation in social welfare, health, housing, defense, regulation of business, and other aspects of the economy. These programs were designed to carry out his pledge in the campaign "to get the country moving." They were well prepared and presented cogent explanations of the proposed reforms, but Congress was not in a mood for reform and most of his proposals were pigeonholed in committee. The inability of the President to secure approval of his legislative program led to a renewed criticism of Congress and demand for its reform.

In the aftermath of the assassination of President Kennedy, President Johnson succeeded in securing the enactment of Kennedy's legislative measures. Elected in 1964 by an overwhelming majority, which swept into office more than 40 liberal Democrats from normally Republican districts, Johnson was able to secure the enactment of his legislative program in 1965. Although he was an experienced and extraordinarily skilled legislative leader, after 1965 he had serious difficulties in securing the enactment of his legislative recommendations.

President Nixon entered office in 1969 without a legislative program and did not submit any measures to the Democratic Congress during the "honeymoon" period that is accorded a new President. In 1970, he submitted 210 legislative proposals in 47 special messages; and Congress passed 97, or 46 percent, principally the least controversial measures.[4] In 1971 he attacked the previous Congress as a "do nothing Congress" that would be remembered not for what it did but what it failed to do, reminiscent of the attack made by President Truman on the Eightieth Congress in the 1948 presidential campaign.

[4] *Congressional Quarterly Weekly Report,* vol. 29, no. 6, Feb. 5, 1971, p. 307.

This review of the successes and failures of the President in securing congressional approval of his legislative program indicates the difficulties that all Presidents face, particularly when one or both houses of Congress are controlled by the opposite party. As Harold J. Laski has written:

> The President is never the master of Congress, except in relatively brief periods of emergency. He does not know that it will accept his principles of action ... even a great majority in both houses is no guarantee of his control. ... Legislation is the main business of both houses. They do not act under instructions of the President; they cooperate with him if they feel so inclined. But they are at every point, save in periods of grave crisis, equal partners with him, and in the event of difference, they, rather than he, are likely to have their way.[5]

CONSTITUTIONAL BASIS The constitutional basis of the President's authority to recommend legislation to Congress is contained in the provision of the Constitution that he "shall from time to time give to the Congress Information of the State of the Union, and recommend to their Consideration such Measures as he shall judge necessary and expedient." Shortly after the opening of each session of Congress, the President delivers his annual message on the State of the Union, and he submits special messages from time to time. Washington delivered his State of the Union message in person, but this practice was discontinued by Jefferson and a hundred years later was revived by Wilson in 1913. The State of the Union message is customarily devoted to a review of the major problems of the country and a statement of the objectives of the administration. Legislative proposals are sent to Congress later, accompanied by special messages explaining their provisions and purposes.

The President also submits to Congress during the first month it is in session two other messages, one accompanying his budget and the other on the national economy. In the budget message, he reviews the fiscal policy and summarizes federal revenues and expenditures. The Economic Report reviews significant trends in the economy and pro-

---

[5] *The American Presidency, an Interpretation,* Harper & Row, Publishers, Incorporated, New York, 1940, pp. 112–113.

vides the background for the President's legislative proposals. The Joint Economic Committee of Congress conducts hearings on the report and issues its own reports on economic trends and problems.

Until about 1820, the President followed the practice of submitting suggested bills with his legislative recommendations, but the practice was discontinued, probably because it was offensive to Congress. It is only within recent years that Congress has accepted without question the Presidential practice of submitting suggested bills with his legislative recommendations, and in some instances congressional committees have insisted upon the submission of specific bills to carry out the President's recommendations.

The third legislative power granted by the Constitution to the President is the veto of bills passed by Congress, subject to being overriden by a two-thirds majority of both houses. Although this power was granted to enable the President to defend his office against encroachments by Congress, it has become one of the most effective means by which the President may influence legislation. The threat of the veto has often enabled the President to secure the removal of provisions in bills to which he strongly objects. Some Presidents have not used the veto power; others have used it only slightly; but the strongest presidents have used it extensively.

INITIATION OF LEGISLATION Why should the President formulate and submit a legislative program to Congress? Members of Congress in the past, overlooking the specific provision of the Constitution directing the President to submit to Congress measures that he deems necessary and expedient, have often maintained that the initiation of legislation is the exclusive function of Congress. The President is the only officer elected by the entire nation; he speaks for the nation and the people look to him to take the leadership in coping with the problems of the country. Each new program and each major change in policies inevitably requires legislation and funds to carry it out. The President is judged today largely on his accomplishments as a legislative leader.

Congress is not organized to formulate a broad, consistent, national legislative program dealing with the problems of the time. Its authority is dispersed among numerous committees and subcommittees, each charged with considering legislation within a particular area. Its outlook is largely local and regional. Many years ago, John Stuart Mill pointed out that the formulation of legislative proposals is not a task for which a large legislative body is fitted.[6] Congress is best qualified to consider the legislation recommended by the President and the executive departments and by its own members.

The President is many men. He has unequaled sources of information, advice, and assistance in the formulation of plans, policies, and legislation dealing with the problems of the nation. He can command the entire resources of the government and has a White House staff of several thousand persons to assist him. Most legislative recommendations originate with the executive departments, which have large staffs of experts, attorneys, and divisions charged with research and planning. The President often creates special commissions of outstanding citizens and experts to inquire into public problems and to formulate recommendations.

The President and his staff do not need to seek out problems that require governmental action. They are constantly brought to his attention by the executive departments, members of Congress, and the leaders of organizations in business, industry, labor, agriculture, and other fields. The President's responsibility is to evaluate these problems and needs, to determine national priorities, and to select those problems for appropriate governmental action that are most urgent and will command wide public support. He must select his programs with great care, choosing those that are economically feasible and politically acceptable, that can be dealt with effectively, and for which the country is prepared for action. The formulation of the necessary legislation requires careful planning, preparation, timing, and consultation with numerous interested groups.

PERSUADING CONGRESS   What means does the President have at his disposal to secure the adoption of his legislative recommendations? His position, of course, is very different from that of the British Prime Minister, who can always count on the votes of party members in Commons. The President must win the votes of members of his party and often some votes from the opposition party in order to secure the

[6] *On Liberty and Considerations on Representative Government,* Basil Blackwell, Oxford, 1948, pp. 168–170.

enactment of his legislative measures. He relies principally on the active support of the party leaders in each house, with whom he usually consults before submitting his recommendations. Often he consults also the chairmen of the committees that will pass upon his bills, who may introduce the bills, thereby assuring that they will be considered by the committee. If the President can gain the enthusiastic support of the party leaders and the committee chairmen, the battle is more than half won.

The President is the head of his party, but his powers to reward those who support his program are limited. He cannot appoint them to high federal office as long as they are members of Congress. He cannot be of much aid to them in being reelected; nor, as President Roosevelt learned in 1938, can he bring about their defeat. He must try to retain their support by acceding to their requests for local projects of benefit to their districts or states as far as possible and by giving them adequate reasons when he is unable to do so. He may use patronage appointments, particularly of federal judges and district attorneys, to maintain their support, but these appointments are not very helpful to the President, for by custom nominees to these offices are selected not by the President but by the senators if they are of the President's party. He therefore must rely heavily on the assistance of the party leaders in Congress in winning the support of party members for his legislative program. Often the President must seek the votes of members of the opposite party to secure the enactment of his bills, and therefore he cannot be too partisan in his appeals.

The President relies heavily upon the support of his own administration, particularly members of the Cabinet and departments that will be in charge of the new program. The head of the department that will administer the proposed program usually takes the lead in winning congressional support. He is the first witness called when the hearings are started. Each department has a liaison staff on the Hill constantly in touch with members of Congress, especially members of committees that pass upon department legislation. As a rule, they are friendly and helpful to the department.

Recent Presidents have used a small staff to assist them in their relations with Congress. The staff serves as a two-way channel of information and communication between the President and members of Congress, keeping him informed of their views and explaining to them his policies. The President's liaison staff must be very diplomatic and astute in approaching members of Congress, who are quick to resent any instruction or attempt at dictation about how they should vote. Members of Congress often feel with reason that they are much better informed about the legislation than the President or his liaison aides.

Finally, the President personally intervenes with members of Congress when necessary to win votes for his bills, telephoning key members to seek their support. He, too, must exercise great care and tact. Those who are not consulted may be offended, and those who are consulted may resent any pressure by the President. But if he makes no effort to secure passage of his bills, he will be criticized by those who have supported his measures for not giving them aid.

The member who introduces a bill is expected to aid in rounding up votes to assure its passage and works closely with administrative personnel who are engaged in lobbying for it. But department officers and members of the President's liaison staff must be careful, in lobbying members of Congress, not to incur any expenditure of public funds, which is prohibited by law. The law was passed in 1919 (41 Stat 68 as amended, U.S.C. Title 18, Sec. 1913) and doubtless was intended to prohibit lobbying by government employees. Although it is not enforced and lobbying by government employees is regularly and openly conducted, an opponent of the proposed legislation may raise a loud hullabaloo if he discovers that public funds are being used.

One of the most effective weapons at the disposal of the President in winning support for his legislative proposals is to carry his appeal to the public. He has access to the media of communication and can go directly to the people by use of television and radio, as well as through press conferences. When the President speaks on national problems, he commands a nationwide audience. Franklin Roosevelt made effective use of the radio in his "fireside chats" to the nation, but he was keenly aware that he could not appear too often or on too many legislative proposals and maintain his support in Congress and the public. Congress will respond to the demands of an aroused public opinion, but appeals to the people over its head are resented by members of Congress and must be used with restraint. John F. Kennedy made effective use of his press conferences, but they did not provide a suitable occasion to explain and defend his legislative proposals. No President has used television interviews more frequently and more effectively than Richard M. Nixon, but they have been used largely to defend his policies with respect to Vietnam and the national economy.

THE CONDUCT
OF INVESTIGATIONS

"We are called the Grand Inquest of the Nation," said William Pitt in the British House of Commons in 1742, "and as such it is our duty to inquire into every step of publick management, either Abroad or at Home, in order to see that nothing has been done amiss." The title may be applied even more appropriately to Congress today, for it devotes much of its time to conducting investigations and watching over the administration. The conduct of investigations has become a major function of Congress, often overshadowing in public attention its legislative activities.[7] Congressional investigations serve several purposes: (1) They provide much of the information that is needed to enact legislation. (2) They enable Congress through its committees to check on the administration of the programs that it has authorized and to hold executive officers responsible. (3) They inform and educate the public and influence public opinion. Congressional investigations cover a very wide range of subjects. The largest number deal with the administration of the executive departments and agencies; some are concerned with important problems of society, such as crime, poverty, slums in our cities, civil rights, automobile safety, water and air pollution, and a host of other subjects; other investigations are concerned with foreign policies, national defense, international organizations, monetary and economic policies. Many investigations deal with subjects of only temporary importance, while others are concerned with the great problems of society.

[7] See Alan Barth, *Government by Investigation*, The Viking Press, Inc., New York, 1955; Telford Taylor, *Grand Inquest: The Story of Congressional Investigations*, Simon and Schuster, Inc., New York, 1955; M. Nelson McGeary, *The Development of Congressional Investigative Power*, Columbia University Press, New York, 1940; Joseph P. Harris, *Congressional Control of Administration*, The Brookings Institution, Washington, D.C., 1964, chap. 9.

HISTORY The first investigation, which was conducted during Washington's first term of office, was to ascertain the reasons for the disastrous defeat of a military expedition. Since that date in 1792, there have been few if any sessions of Congress that did not witness one or more investigations of the conduct of the executive departments. At present Congress conducts more than 100 separate investigations at each session of Congress and innumerable inquiries into the administration of the departments. Under their authority to exercise "oversight of the executive departments," standing committees and their staffs are constantly conducting inquiries into administration.

Before 1946, Congress conducted relatively few investigations. A special resolution was required by each house to authorize the conduct of an investigation, and usually a special committee was appointed to conduct the investigation. When the same party controlled the Presidency and the House of Representatives, the majority-party leaders of the House could usually be relied upon to block any investigation that might prove to be embarrassing to the administration. In the Senate, however, where the rules permitted unlimited debate, the party leaders were less able to block proposed investigations of the executive departments. Senators demanding an investigation could continue their criticism of a department and demand its investigation until the party leaders consented. For this reason, the Senate rather than the House has conducted most of the investigations of the government. Following the two world wars and at other times when Congress was under control of the party opposed to the President, numerous investigations were instituted, primarily to gain partisan advantage.

The control formerly exercised by the party leaders over the institution of investigations was largely ended by the Legislative Reorganization Act of 1946, which authorized all standing committees to conduct investigations of government agencies or subjects within their respective jurisdictions, and provided for an annual appropriation of $10,000 to each committee for this purpose. Many committees today spend far larger sums on investigations, which are voted in supplemental appropriations. In addition, the Congressional Reorganization Act of 1946 created a Government Operations Committee in each house; the committees are given authority to investigate executive departments and agencies throughout the government. This act thus opened the floodgates for congressional investigations, which have since multiplied and enormously increased in cost. Formerly, most investigations were initiated by the party opposing the President or by opponents within his own party, but today they are often initiated by members of the President's party.

PURPOSES Investigations provide one of the most powerful weapons of Congress. They may be used to ferret out mismanagement or administrative abuses and to force the executive department to make needed improvements. Inquiries into important social and economic problems may be used to inform and arouse public opinion and pave the way for corrective legislation. Congress has often used investigations to expose practices and conditions that warrant public attention and concern, as, for example, the Kefauver committee investigation of organized crime in the 1950s. A widely publicized Senate investigation of automobile safety in 1966 led to the enactment of federal legislation imposing safety standards, although before the hearings there was little public interest or support of such legislation. Several years ago, a congressional investigation of the marketing of harmful drugs aroused public opinion and led to the enactment of legislation strengthening the Federal Pure Food and Drug Act, although earlier efforts over a number of years to strengthen the law and its enforcement had been unsuccessful.

Congressional investigations are often conducted to inform and educate the public when no legislation is contemplated. A good example is the hearings conducted in 1966 and 1967 by Sen. William Fulbright, chairman of the Senate Foreign Relations Committee, on the foreign policy of the administration, particularly our involvement in the Vietnam war. These hearings provided a nationwide forum, not only for administration spokesmen, but also for highly informed and responsible critics; and they were influential in the mounting public criticism of the war and demand for a negotiated peace.

The House Un-American Activities Committee (now the Internal Security Committee), created in 1938, is an example of a committee whose primary and practically sole function is to conduct investigations, not with a view to legislation but rather to inform the public of the dangers of subversive organizations and groups, particularly the

Communist conspiracy. Many of the criticisms of congressional investigations can be laid at the door of this committee, which as been widely censured for smearing witnesses and depriving them of their constitutional rights without giving them any real opportunity to defend themselves. In its controversial history of more than a quarter of a century, the committee has proposed only two or three relatively unimportant bills.

Investigations of the administration of the executive departments have become a major part of the work of congressional committees and subcommittees, in many instances requiring as much time and effort as consideration of legislation. Formerly, such investigations were conducted sporadically by special investigating committees following charges of mismanagement, official misconduct, or misuse of public funds, but today conducting investigations is a recognized function of all standing legislative committees. Committee inquiries are seldom concerned with charges of flagrant mismanagement or misconduct of executive officers, but rather with the problems, policies, results, and administration of particular programs or activities that have been criticized, and in search for needed improvements, economies, and possible changes in legislation.

Because of the tremendous growth of the functions of the federal government during the past 40 years and the increasingly technical nature of federal programs, Congress has of necessity delegated greater power and authority to executive officers than formerly. The initiative in proposing legislation, formerly regarded as an exclusive congressional prerogative, has largely passed to executive officers. Because of the great increase in executive power, Congress has sought to restore the historic balance between the two branches of government by strengthening its control over administration by the executive departments. This is accomplished largely through investigations.

Committee inquiries into administration are essential if Congress is to legislate wisely on the vast government programs. They are equally essential if it is to hold executive officers responsible for efficient and economical management of the executive departments and agencies. The possibility of a congressional investigation provides a safeguard—but not the only one—against executive mismanagement and abuses of authority. Yet it should be pointed out that legislative investigations, if carried too far or made too often, may have unfortunate results, particularly if the investigators attempt to dictate executive decisions. The fear of an investigation may enfeeble administration, causing executive officers to become timid where they should be bold in taking needed actions, fearful of accepting responsibility or initiating needed improvements and innovations. An excessive amount of "looking over the shoulders" of executive officers is not conducive to vigorous, efficient administration, which is sorely needed in government programs. The Joint Committee of Congress on the Conduct of the War Between the States in 1861 to 1865 is perhaps the best example of the harmful effects of meddling by a legislative investigating committee. It attempted to direct the President in the prosecution of the war, dictate appointments of commanding generals, and demanded to be informed on future military plans, which President Lincoln refused to reveal. Lincoln called the committee a "marplot," declaring that "its greatest purpose seems to be to hamper my actions and obstruct military operations."[8] The McCarthy investigations of the State Department in the 1950s disrupted its operations, weakened the morale of its staff, and did untold damage to an important arm of the government when this country was engaged in a worldwide struggle with Communism.

There are numerous examples of congressional investigations that exposed mismanagement and wrongdoing of officials in the executive departments at a time when their responsible officers failed to take any action. The celebrated Teapot Dome investigations of the 1920s exposed huge frauds in the Harding administration, forced the retirement of several members of the President's Cabinet, and were followed by the conviction of a number of high federal executive officials. The investigations by the Truman committee of procurement of military supplies, industrial mobilization, and related problems during World War II made a great contribution and undoubtedly resulted in great savings. An investigation of the Internal Revenue Service during the Truman administration led to its reorganization and reform, taking the collectors of internal revenue out of politics, as well as resulting in the prosecution of several collectors for frauds and official misconduct. The investigation of regulatory commissions during the Eisenhow-

[8] See Joseph P. Harris, *Congressional Control of Administration*, The Brookings Institution, Washington, D.C., 1964, pp. 253-255.

er administration exposed improper political influence on the work of these commissions and led to the resignation of Sherman Adams, the President's chief adviser and assistant. Congressional committees today are constantly inquiring into the management practices and administration of all departments, especially defense, foreign aid, and other programs that have been criticized.

Each house also conducts sporadic investigations of campaign expenditures and election practices. Occasionally, investigations are made of charges of misconduct of its own members, but few members have ever been removed or even censured. Congress, which is often highly critical of unethical practices or conflicts of interest on the part of executive officers, is notoriously tolerant of the conduct of its own members. Each house has recently created an ethics committee, but it remains to be seen how effective they will be.

LEGALITY The authority of Congress to conduct investigations incident to legislation has never been questioned. The Supreme Court decided in 1880 in the case of *Kilbourn v. Thompson* (103 U.S. 68) that Congress did not have power to conduct investigations unrelated to legislation. This ruling, however, was modified by later decisions that increased the scope of permissible investigations. In *McGrain v. Daugherty* (273 U.S. 135), the Supreme Court in 1927 upheld the power of a Senate committee to inquire into the private financial affairs of a Cabinet member.

The authority of congressional committees to require witnesses to testify as to their political beliefs and associations, particularly whether they are or formerly were members of the Communist party, and to disclose the names of other persons whom they believe to have been Communists, has frequently been challenged in the courts. Witnesses may avoid answering such questions by pleading their rights under the Fifth Amendment, which provides that "no person . . . shall be compelled in any criminal case to be a witness against himself." Most persons, however, are reluctant to enter this plea, which is popularly regarded as a confession of guilt. Many witnesses who were willing to testify as to whether they are or formerly were members of the Communist party have entered the plea of the Fifth Amendment in order to avoid testifying concerning the political beliefs and associations of others.

In the case of *Watkins v. United States* [354 U.S. 178 (1957)], Watkins testified that he had never been a member of the Communist party but declined to testify as to other individuals, pleading that the House Un-American Activities Committee did not have the right under the First Amendment, which guarantees freedom of speech and assembly, to require him to answer such questions. The Supreme Court sustained his plea, holding that Congress has no general authority to expose the private affairs of individuals without justification in terms of the functions of Congress. The Court held that without specific legislative authorization, a committee cannot legally require a witness to answer questions about his beliefs and associations unless such questions are clearly relevant to the purpose of the inquiry. Two years later, however, the Supreme Court held in the case of *Barenblatt v. U.S.* [360 U.S. 109 (1959)] that a committee inquiring into Communism in education could require Barenblatt, a former assistant at the University of Michigan, to testify whether he had been a member of the Communist party. A majority of the Court held that the question was relevant to the inquiry.

Another issue that has frequently arisen relates to the power of the President and the departments, acting under his instructions, to withhold confidential papers called for by congressional committees. The rights of the President to withhold such information and to instruct the departments not to furnish confidential papers is well established and has been exercised by practically all Presidents since Washington's time.

CRITICISMS AND PROPOSED REFORMS   Many criticisms have been voiced of congressional investigations in recent years, especially because of the excesses of a few committees. The investigations of Senator McCarthy in 1953 seriously injured our prestige and relations with other countries at a time when the country was engaged in a bitter struggle with Communism. They created a wave of hysteria throughout the country and lowered the morale of the federal service, especially in the State Department. During the height of the McCarthy investigations, Walter Lippmann warned that unless congressional investigations were curbed they would bring about a fundamental change in the Constitution. (See the account of the McCarthy investigations in Chapter 1.) The investigations conducted by the House Un-

American Activities Committee (now the Internal Security Committee) were strongly criticized for the denial of the constitutional rights of witnesses. It cannot be doubted that serious harm was done to the security of the country by some investigations that professed to safeguard it. Thoughtful citizens deplore some of the tactics used by the committee and its violation of the rights of witnesses. Others have defended the committee on the ground that these tactics are necessary to expose the Communist conspiracy. The House of Representatives adopted a code of procedure for its committees in 1955 that is designed to prevent some of the actions that have been most criticized in the past, and several of the Senate committees have adopted similar rules of procedure, which are intended to assure witnesses of their rights. But there is no effective way to enforce such rules. Some of the investigations most criticized for violating individual rights have been conducted by committees with admirable rules of procedure.

The major criticisms voiced against congressional investigations include the following: (1) Investigations are often inspired by partisan or factional reasons and are undertaken, not to ascertain the facts and to recommend legislation, but rather to embarrass the party in power. (2) Because of partisanship, they are often conducted in a biased manner and do not win the confidence of Congress and the public. (3) They are expensive, disruptive of administration, and often fail to bring about needed improvements. (4) They are usually inefficient because members of Congress seldom have the expert knowledge or sufficient time to conduct a thorough inquiry. (5) Congress conducts too many investigations, often aimed at securing publicity rather than facts. Many investigations are conducted to advance a particular policy desired by its sponsors. For example, the late Sen. Patrick A. McCarran of Nevada conducted an investigation intermittently from 1941 to 1947, the purpose of which was to prevent the Interior Department from raising grazing fees.

One of the major reforms proposed is that Congress make greater use of citizen investigating commissions, whose members may be carefully selected for their qualifications and removed from partisan politics. The British government has long used royal commissions to inquire into many of the great problems of society that require legislative action, and Parliament itself, which, as already mentioned, was called the "Grand Inquest," seldom conducts such inquiries. Congress has not shown any enthusiasm for delegating its investigative powers to other bodies, though it has at times created such investigating commissions as, for example, the two Hoover Commissions, which were joint legislative-executive bodies with citizen representation. In recent decades, increasing use has been made of presidential commissions, which correspond to the royal commissions in Great Britain, to conduct inquiries into major public needs and problems.

THE POWER OF THE PURSE

The "power of the purse"[9] is granted to Congress by Article I of the Constitution, which authorizes it "to lay and collect Taxes, Duties, Imposts, and Excises," and provides that "No Money shall be drawn from the Treasury, but in Consequence of Appropriations by Law." Through this power, Congress controls government finances and exercises its most systematic and effective control over the administration of the executive departments, which today is one of its most important functions. Historically, the power of the purse was the first power exercised by legislative bodies, preceding the power to enact laws.

The powers of Congress over finance are exercised through four types of laws: (1) laws levying taxes, (2) laws authorizing the incurring of debt, (3) laws authorizing government activities and programs and the expenditures involved, and (4) appropriation acts. Revenue and debt legislation is assigned to the Ways and Means Committee of the House and the Finance Committee of the Senate; appropriations are passed on by the appropriations committees of the two houses; and acts authorizing government programs are reported by the various legislative committees for departments and agencies within their jurisdictions. It is apparent that the responsibility for finance legislation is divided among practically all the standing committees and subcommit-

[9]See Aaron Wildavsky, *The Politics of the Budgetary Process,* Little, Brown and Company, Boston, 1964; Frederic Mosher, *Program Budgeting: Theory and Practice,* Public Administration Service, Chicago, 1954; Arthur Smithies, *The Budgetary Process in the United States,* McGraw-Hill Book Company, New York, 1955; Joseph P. Harris, *Congressional Control of Administration,* The Brookings Institution, Washington, D.C., 1964, chaps. 3–6; Committee for Economic Development, *Making Congress More Effective,* New York, 1970, chap. 2.

tees of each house, a major weakness of Congress in exercising its responsibility for the fiscal policies of the government. To divide responsibility for the financial decisions of the government among 300 separate committees and subcommittees of the two houses is to destroy it.

In this section we shall examine the organization and procedures used by Congress in passing on the President's expenditure budget. It is through the expenditure budget that Congress reviews and passes on not only the departments' budgets but also their programs, operations, and policies. Through appropriations, Congress allocates available resources among the competing government programs—one of its most important policy decisions.

APPROPRIATIONS AND LEGISLATION Appropriations may be voted only for government activities or programs that have been authorized by legislation. As a consequence, all standing legislative committees have an important role in determining the purposes for which federal funds may be spent and, in many cases, the maximum amount that may be spent for the program. If a new type of insect threatens potato crops, before the Department of Agriculture can undertake a program of eradication and control, legislation must be enacted to authorize the expenditure of federal funds for this purpose. Such legislation usually specifies the objectives of the program, prescribes the major policies to be followed, authorizes expenditures for personnel and other items, and may limit the expenditures that may be made for this purpose.

It is sometimes said that the legislative committees pass upon the policies involved in government programs and the appropriations committees pass upon the funds, but this is an oversimplification. In determining the funds to be appropriated for each program, the appropriations committees work within a framework of policies laid down by the authorizing legislation, but within this framework they make many important policy decisions. In addition, they exercise constant supervision and oversight of the activities of the departments. Their control is potent, for "he who pays the piper, calls the tune."

The dual system of *authorizing* government programs and *appropriating* funds for their support inevitably results in a division of responsibility for the financing of government activities. The legislative committees that recommend the legislation authorizing government programs have no direct responsibility for the finances of the government. They are usually the advocates of the particular government programs upon which they pass. As a result, legislation authorizing new programs is often passed with little attention to the availability of funds and the needs of other programs. Once the authorizing legislation is enacted, the department concerned is, in effect, directed to submit a budget to carry out the program, the President is under obligation to include funds in his budget, and the appropriations committees are expected to vote funds to carry out the program. In the Senate, the actions of the legislative committees and the Appropriations Committee are coordinated by considerable overlapping of membership; but, in the House, members of the Appropriations Committee are not permitted to serve on other committees and differences of opinion are not uncommon.

THE HOUSE APPROPRIATIONS COMMITTEE The Appropriations Committee is usually regarded as the most powerful committee of each house, though not necessarily the first in member preference and prestige. Assignment to the appropriations committees is much sought after because of the power that the committee wields. "Where the money is, that's where the power is," writes one student of the House Appropriations Committee in summing up the feelings of members. "They prize their ability to reward or punish other participants in the political process—executive officials, fellow Congressmen, constituents, and other clientele groups."[10]

The chairmen and ranking members of the Appropriations subcommittees have great influence on the actions of the departments whose budgets they pass upon, especially with respect to matters affecting their own districts. "The predominant view that agency officials have of these legislators," wrote Aaron Wildavsky, another student of the appropriations process, "is that they are very powerful people. They can do you a world of good and they can cut your throat." A State Department official was quoted as saying, "Let's face it. When Rooney (chairman of the appropriations subcommittee) whistles, we've

[10] Richard F. Fenno, "The House Appropriations Committee as a Political System," *American Political Science Review,* vol. 56, p. 314, June, 1962.

just got to dance."[11] To the Appropriations Committee members come not only the executive officers seeking approval of their budget requests but also members of Congress seeking appropriations for projects in their districts that they need in order to be reelected.

The House Appropriations Committee consists of 50 members, the largest committee of the House. The work of the committee is done almost entirely by 14 subcommittees, each assigned a department or group of departments and agencies. Ordinarily members are not appointed to the committee until after they have served at least two terms. Most members come from safe districts and usually serve on the committee for many years. In 1961, the average length of service in Congress of the 50 members of the House Appropriations Committee was 13.1 years, and the average length of service on the committee was 9.3 years.[12] The chairmen and ranking senior members of subcommittees, who take the leading part in their work, have usually served on the committee for 15 years or more.

The House appropriations subcommittees conduct daily hearings on the department budgets, extending usually over several months. The members are noted for hard work, regular attendance at subcommittee meetings, and high esprit de corps. They regard themselves as the "protectors of the federal treasury" and are invariably critical of the "other house" for its liberality in restoring cuts made by the House. Typical comments of members are: "It's a tradition of the Appropriations Committee to cut. It's ingrained in you from the time you get on the committee." "There has never been a budget submitted to Congress that couldn't be cut." "No subcommittee of which I have been a member has ever reported out a bill without a cut in the budget. I am *proud* of that record."[13] A study of the record of the House Appropriations Committee in passing on the budgets of 37 bureaus over a period of 12 years indicates that reductions were made in 77 percent of the bureau budgets. In many instances, however, it should be noted that the cuts were restored at least in part by the Senate, which often votes more money than requested in the President's budget; and many reductions were later restored in supplemental and deficiency

---

[11] Wildavsky, *The Politics of the Budgetary Process,* p. 54.

[12] Fenno, "The House Appropriations Committe . . . ," p. 312.

[13] *Ibid.*

appropriations. The commonly accepted idea that Congress reduces federal expenditures is largely a myth. The prevailing drives in Congress are for greater rather than less expenditures.

It would be a mistake to assume that budgets are invariably cut by the Appropriations Committee, or that they should be. Members of the committee usually are ambivalent; they seek generally to make cuts in the department budgets, but they fight for appropriations of benefit to their own districts. This is understood and accepted by other members. The budgets of departments or agencies that have strong political or clientele support are usually adopted with few, if any, cuts. The House subcommittee on Agriculture, for example, which consists almost exclusively of members from predominantly agricultural districts, seldom reduces the estimates for agricultural programs, which have strong clientele support. The FBI and the National Institute of Health have such strong support in Congress that their budgets are rarely cut and are often increased. Appropriations Committee members, like other members of Congress, often fight for appropriations for programs that they favor. "I am proud," said one member, "of the fact that 16 years ago I was fighting to increase in this very room the money set aside for soil conservation."[14]

The appropriations subcommittees are largely autonomous, subject to relatively little direction and control by the full committee. Each subcommittee is jealous of its authority and resists any change in its action by the committee. Through long service on the same subcommittee, members acquire a high degree of expertness and knowledge of the work and budgets of the particular departments; and there is a widespread feeling that only members who have attended the lengthy subcommittee hearings and the subsequent "mark-up" of the appropriations bill are qualified to pass upon the budget estimates of the department. Under the custom of reciprocity, members of each subcommittee approve the bills of other subcommittees and expect similar treatment of their own bills. As a result, the Appropriations Committee ordinarily approves the bills and reports submitted by its subcommittees without change and usually without detailed review. In no other area of legislation does Congress delegate decision making so

[14] Wildavsky, *The Politics of the Budgetary Process,* p. 49.

largely to the few specialists who are members of the subcommittee that reported the bill.

The subcommittee reviews of the department budgets are noted for the absence of partisanship. After the differences among members are compromised, usually the bill and the attending report have the unanimous support of subcommittee members. At times it is the members of the President's party who lead the efforts to reduce his budget. For example, Rep. Otto E. Passman, Democrat of Louisiana, chairman of the House Appropriations Subcommittee on Foreign Operations, has long been a leading opponent of foreign aid appropriations, which his subcommittee has regularly slashed.

The House appropriations subcommittee hearings are ordinarily conducted behind closed doors, attended only by members of the committee, its staff, and witnesses from the executive department or agency whose budget is being considered. Even other members of Congress are not permitted to attend subcommittee hearings, except public hearings that are held to permit other members of Congress to testify in support of appropriations of benefit to their own districts. Representatives of taxpayers' organizations and other groups are also given opportunity to make statements at public hearings but not to attend closed hearings. With rare exception, those who testify are in favor of increased appropriations for activities in which they are interested. Though taxpayers' organizations urge economy, few witnesses ever appear opposing appropriations or seeking reductions of particular appropriation items.

The examination of departmental budgets conducted by the subcommittees is historical and cumulative. Each subcommittee has passed upon the budgets of the same department in previous years and usually concentrates its attention primarily on requests for additional personnel and any proposed new activities. Little attempt is made to review the entire department budget and work programs; but any item, old or new, is subject to examination and interrogation. The departments submit voluminous "justification books" describing their entire operations, work programs, results of past years, and other information, which the committee members and staff examine to find "soft spots" for further interrogation.

Department witnesses are required by executive order to support the budget estimates submitted by the President, which are usually substantially less than those originally requested by the department. Occasionally, a department may seek through friends on the subcommittee to secure a larger appropriation than requested in the President's budget, but such action is sure to incur the displeasure of the President and the powerful Bureau of the Budget and is seldom attempted.

After the hearings are concluded, the subcommittee meets in executive session with its staff to "mark up" the appropriations bill. In determining the amounts to be allowed for each budget item and activity, the subcommittee takes into account many different factors, such as the results of the program in previous years, the extent of public support, attitudes of members of Congress, possible economies, and whether the department plans are well designed to accomplish the objectives. The evaluation of these and other factors by the subcommittees may be different from that of the President and the executive department, who look at government programs from a national viewpoint, while members of Congress are more locally oriented. This is one of the reasons why a legislative review is so necessary and important in a democratic government.

Appropriations bills are submitted to the full committee for its approval, after which they are reported to the House with a report that summarizes the major provisions of the bill, the changes that have been made in the President's budget, and often includes policy directives to the departments. Although these directives are not voted on by either house and have no legal effect, their practical effect is about the same on the department as though they were enacted into law. During the hearings, the members of the subcommittee often give oral instruction to department officials and reach an understanding with them about future policies and actions. The appropriations subcommittees often instruct the department officials to consult with them before taking certain actions for which funds are provided, and they exercise a continuous oversight of the work of the departments and agencies whose budgets they pass upon.

When an appropriations bill is considered by the House, there is first a brief general debate on the bill, following which the House resolves itself into the committee of the whole. The Speaker leaves the chair, designating another member to serve as chairman, and the bill is taken up section by section under the five-minutes rule. Amendments are offered from the floor, but few are adopted except those brought in by the Appropriations Committee. Amendments to increase certain items of benefit to a particular district or area, such as an appropriation for a hospital, are often proposed but seldom adopted. They are strongly opposed by the members of the Appropriations Committee because if an amendment of this type is passed, it will open the floodgate for many other similar amendments.

THE SENATE APPROPRIATIONS COMMITTEE   The Senate Appropriations Committee does not ordinarily consider department budgets until it receives the appropriations bills that have been passed by the House, and then it acts largely as an appeals body. The appropriations subcommittees in the Senate usually confine their attention to requests by the departments to restore, at least in part, the cuts made by the House. Contrary to the practice in the House, the Senate appropriations subcommittees usually conduct public hearings on the department budgets. Usually, only the chairman and one or two other members are present. Most members of the Senate Appropriations Committee serve on several subcommittees, in addition to their other committee and subcommittee assignments, and hence are often unable to attend subcommittee hearings because of conflicts. All members, however, participate in the decisions of the subcommittee of which they are members, regardless of whether they have attended its hearings, and under the practice of "senatorial courtesy," their wishes are usually followed with respect to appropriations for projects in their own states.

Members of the Senate Appropriations Committee do not consider that their primary function is to cut department budget estimates, but rather to consider the financial needs of the department and to provide funds to maintain the level of service demanded by the public. Since senators are also members of legislative committees, contrary to the practice in the House, they are usually well informed about the programs and activities of the departments whose budgets they pass upon. It is not surprising that the Senate often restores at least a part of the cuts voted by the House and sometimes votes larger funds than requested by the President. The House often reduces the department's budget, knowing that its cuts will probably be restored by the Senate. On the other hand, the Senate votes increases, knowing that they will in all probability be reduced by the conference committee.

As in the House, the Senate Appropriations Committee ordinarily approves the appropriations bills and reports submitted by its subcommittees without change. Appropriations bills are seldom debated at length in the Senate, although appropriations for controversial items, such as foreign aid, may lead to a spirited debate. It is not uncommon for huge appropriations of billions of dollars to be voted with virtually no debate. The twenty or more appropriations bills, which are passed piecemeal at different times, do not provide an occasion for a general debate on the fiscal policies of the government. This is regrettable, for such a debate would afford the minority party an opportunity to attack the fiscal policies of the government and would require the majority party leaders to defend them, thus establishing greater responsibility for the budget as a whole.

After an appropriations bill has passed both houses, it is customarily sent to a conference committee to compromise the differences. The presiding officer of each house appoints its members (or managers, as they are called) of the conference committee, who usually include the chairman and ranking minority party member of the Appropriations Committee, the chairman and ranking minority member of the subcommittee, and possibly two or more other senior members. The conference committee usually meets with a sense of urgency, for the fiscal year when the funds are needed is near at hand, or, indeed, may have already started. Each side yields on items that it considers of lesser importance in return for similar concessions by the other house; some differences are compromised by agreeing upon a midway figure between the amounts voted by the two houses. Occasionally one house may object strongly to certain provisions in the language of the appropriations acts as passed by the other house, and a temporary deadlock may ensue. Formerly, Congress usually passed the appropriation bills before the beginning (July 1) of the fiscal year to which they applied, but in recent years appropriation bills are often not passed until several months after the start of the fiscal year. In 1969, Congress did not pass any appropriation bills until October; and, when it adjourned in December, two major appropriation bills had not yet been passed. One was not passed until March, 1970, eight months after the beginning of the fiscal year to which it applied. These delays seriously handicap orderly and efficient administration.

CRITICISMS The major criticism of the congressional budgetary process is that Congress does not consider and act upon the budget as a whole but instead passes 20 or more appropriations bills annually, as well as separate tax and debt legislation. The President considers the budget as a whole, including estimated revenues and proposed new taxes as well as the expenditure estimates of the departments. In preparing his budget, he also considers economic trends, the outlook, and the impact of the federal budget on the economy. Because of the great size of the federal budget today, economic considerations are highly important. Congress, however, divides the President's budget into a dozen or more parts, assigns each to a separate committee or subcommittee for consideration, and acts upon their bills piecemeal. This procedure is contrary to sound budgetary practice, which would require the legislature as well as the executive to consider and pass upon the budget at one time, in order to decide upon appropriations for each major governmental activity when it is known what the requirements of other governmental activities are and whether the available revenues will be sufficient to meet these requirements.

Obviously the present organization and procedures of Congress do not provide for consideration of the budget as a whole and the allocation of funds for governmental activities on the basis of a comparison and evaluation of their respective needs and values to the public. Responsibility for considering the budget and recommending appropriations and revenues is badly divided among different committees and subcommittees, which often act independently of each other.

The Committee for Economic Development, after making a careful study of congressional review and control of finance, made the following criticisms of its organization and procedures and recommended five major improvements.

The present Congressional approach to fiscal affairs is indefensible. When budget decisions are extended long past the beginning of the fiscal year for which they are intended, when there is no Congressional mechanism to tie revenues and appropriations into a coherent pattern, when no legislative procedure exists to initiate actions based on a comprehensive view of the economy, then national stability is endangered. . . . To correct these conditions we recommend that:

Means for a comprehensive review of the annual budget be established and used, relating total revenues and expenditures to the state of the economy.

Annual authorizations be discontinued; instead, authorizations should be made along program and project lines, fully funded for a minimum term of four years.

Evaluation of program performance, in terms of objectives as well as dollars, be heavily stressed.

The federal fiscal year be changed to coincide with the calendar year, so that appropriations may always precede expenditures.

Congress establish and observe deadline dates for both authorizations and appropriations.[15]

REVIEW QUESTIONS

1. Why has the initiative of legislation largely passed from Congress to the President and the executive departments?

2. What means does the President have to secure the passage of his bills? Discuss each.

3. For what purposes does Congress conduct investigations? How effectively do they serve these purposes? Discuss.

4. Why have congressional investigations greatly increased since 1940?

5. Discuss the major criticisms and proposed reforms of congressional investigations.

6. What are the different ways in which Congress exercises "the power of the purse"? Discuss the differences between *authorization* and *appropriation*.

7. Discuss the different roles and attitudes of members of the House and the Senate in passing on the budget.

8. What are the major criticisms of the congressional review of the budget? How could it be strengthened?

[15] *Making Congress More Effective,* p. 18.

FOR FURTHER READING

Acheson, Dean: *A Citizen Looks at Congress,* Harper & Row, Publishers, Incorporated, New York, 1956.

Bailey, Stephen K.: *Congress Makes a Law,* Columbia University Press, New York, 1950.

Barber, James J.: *The Lawmakers: Recruitment and Adaptation to Legislative Life,* Yale University Press, New Haven, Conn., 1965.

Barth, Alan: *Government by Investigation,* The Viking Press, Inc., New York, 1955.

Berman, Daniel M.: *A Bill Becomes a Law,* The Macmillan Company, New York, 1962.

————: *In Congress Assembled,* The Macmillan Company, New York, 1964.

Bibby, John, and Roger Davidson: *On Capitol Hill: Studies in the Legislative Process,* Holt, Rinehart and Winston, Inc., New York, 1967.

Bolling, Richard: *House Out of Order,* E. P. Dutton & Co., Inc., New York, 1965.

Burns, James Macgregor: *The Deadlock of Democracy: Four Party Politics in America,* Prentice-Hall, Inc., Englewood Cliffs, N.J., 1963.

Clapp, Charles L.: *The Congressman: His Work as He Sees It,* The Brookings Institution, Washington, D.C., 1963.

Clark, Joseph S. (ed.): *Congressional Reform: Problems and Prospects,* Thomas Y. Crowell Company, New York, 1965.

————: *Congress: The Sapless Branch,* Harper & Row, Publishers, Incorporated, New York, 1965.

Cleaveland, Frederick N., and Associates: *Congress and Urban Problems,* The Brookings Institution, Washington, D.C., 1969.

Committee for Economic Development, *Making Congress More Effective,* New York, 1970.

Cummings, Milton C., *Congressmen and the Electorate,* The Free Press, New York, 1966.

Davidson, Roger H.: *The Role of the Congressman,* Pegasus, New York, 1969.

————, David M. Kovenock, and Michael K. O'Leary: *Congress in Crisis: Politics and Congressional Reform,* Wadsworth Publishing Co., Inc., Belmont, Calif., 1966.

Dixon, Robert G.: *Democratic Representation: Reapportionment in Law and Politics,* Oxford University Press, Fair Lawn, N.J., 1968.

Eidenberg, Eugene, and Roy D. Morley: *An Act of Congress: The Legislative Process and the Making of Educational Policy,* W. W. Norton & Company, Inc., New York, 1969.

Froman, Lewis A., Jr.: *The Congressional Process,* Little, Brown and Company, Boston, 1967.

Galloway, George B.: *The Legislative Process in Congress,* Thomas Y. Crowell Company, New York, 1953.

————: *History of the United States House of Representatives,* Thomas Y. Crowell Company, New York, 1961.

Griffith, Ernest S.: *Congress: Its Contemporary Role,* New York University Press, New York, 1951.

Gross, Bertram: *The Legislative Struggle,* McGraw-Hill Book Company, New York, 1953.

Harris, Joseph P.: *The Advice and Consent of the Senate,* University of California Press, Berkeley, 1953.

————: *Congressional Control of Administration,* The Brookings Institution, Washington, D.C., 1964.

Haynes, George H.: *The Senate of the United States,* 2 vols., Houghton Mifflin Company, Boston, 1938.

Huitt, Ralph K., and Robert L. Peabody: *Congress: Two Decades of Analysis,* Harper & Row, Publishers, Incorporated, New York, 1969.

Jones, Charles O.: *Party and Policy Making: The House Republican Policy Committee,* Rutgers University Press, New Brunswick, N.J., 1964.

Kofmehl, Kenneth: *Professional Staffs of Congress,* Purdue University Press, Lafayette, Ind., 1962.

Lowi, Theodore J. (ed.): *Legislative Politics, U.S.A.,* 2d ed., Little, Brown and Company, Boston, 1965.

MacNeil, Neil: *Forge of Democracy: The House of Representatives,* David McKay Company, Inc., New York, 1963.

McKay, Robert B.: *Reapportionment: The Law and Politics of Equal Representation,* The Twentieth Century Fund, New York, 1965.

Matthews, Donald R.: *U.S. Senators and Their World,* The University of North Carolina Press, Chapel Hill, 1960.

Mayhew, David R.: *Party Loyalty among Congressmen,* Harvard University Press, Cambridge, Mass., 1966.

Miller, Clem: *Member of the House,* Charles Scribner's Sons, New York, 1962.

Morrow, William L.: *Congressional Committees,* Charles Scribner's Sons, New York, 1969.

Peabody, Robert L., and Nelson W. Polsby (eds.): *New Perspectives on the House of Representatives,* Rand McNally & Company, Chicago, 1963.

Pettit, Lawrence K., and Edward Keynes (eds.): *The Legislative Process in the U.S. Senate,* Rand McNally & Company, Chicago, 1969.

Rieselbach, Leroy N. (ed.): *The Congressional System: Notes and Readings,* Wadsworth Publishing Co., Inc., Belmont, California, 1970.

Ripley, Randall B.: *Party Leaders in the House of Representatives,* The Brookings Institution, Washington, D.C., 1967.

Robinson, James A.: *The House Rules Committee,* The Bobbs-Merrill Company, Inc., Indianapolis, 1963.

Saloma, John S. III: *Congress and the New Politics,* Little, Brown and Company, Boston, 1969.

Scott, Andrew M., and Margaret A. Hunt: *Congress and Lobbies,* University of North Carolina Press, Chapel Hill, 1966.

Steiner, Gilbert Y.: *The Congressional Conference Committee,* The University of Illinois Press, Urbana, 1951.

Taylor, Telford: *Grand Inquest: The Story of Congressional Investigations,* Simon and Schuster, Inc., New York, 1955.

Tacheron, Donald G., and Morris K. Udall: *The Job of the Congressman,* The Bobbs-Merrill Company, Inc., Indianapolis, 1966.

Truman, David: *The Congressional Party,* John Wiley & Sons, Inc., New York, 1959.

——— (ed.): *The Congress and America's Future,* Prentice-Hall, Inc., Englewood Cliffs, N.J., 1965.

White, William S.: *Citadel: The Story of the U.S. Senate,* Harper & Row, Publishers, Incorporated, New York, 1956.

Young, Roland: *The American Congress,* Harper & Row, Publishers, Incorporated, New York, 1958.

INDEX

189